THE
IRISH COUNTRYWOMEN'S ASSOCIATION
BOOK OF BREAD AND BAKING

About the ICA

Founded in May 1910, the aim of the Irish Countrywomen's Association (ICA) was 'to improve the standard of life in rural Ireland through education and co-operative effort'. Today the ICA has 475 local Guilds in cities, towns and rural areas throughout Ireland. They continue to offer support and fun as well as opportunities to make friends, learn new skills and contribute to the wider community. Every day, the women share with each other nuggets of advice, tried-and-tested recipes and practical help, and they hope this book will pass on some of that knowledge to you. This book's predecessors, *The ICA Cookbook, The ICA Book of Home and Family, The ICA Book of Tea and Company* and *The ICA Book of Christmas*, were all bestsellers in Ireland and overseas.

THE IRISH COUNTRYWOMEN'S ASSOCIATION BOOK OF BREAD AND BAKING

General Editor Aoife Carrigy

GILL BOOKS

GILL BOOKS
Hume Avenue
Park West
Dublin 12
www.gillbooks.ie

Gill Books is an imprint of M.H. Gill and Co.

978 0 7171 8424 8

General Editor Aoife Carrigy

Design and print origination by Tanya M Ross, Elementinc.ie
Illustrations by Tanya M Ross, Elementinc.ie

Photography © Leo Byrne
Styled by Charlotte O'Connell
Printed by Edelvives, Spain

Recipe testing by Erica Drum
Copy-edited by Susan McKeever
Index compiled by Eileen O'Neill

This book is typeset in Lora 8.5pt on 12pt and Verlag 10pt on 12pt.
The paper used in this book comes from the wood pulp of managed forests. For every tree felled, at least one tree is planted, thereby renewing natural resources.

A CIP catalogue record for this book is available from the British Library.

5 4 3 2 1

Contents

CHAPTER 3: SAVOURY BREADS

CHAPTER 4: SCONES, BREAD ROLLS & CRACKERS

CHAPTER 5: BISCUITS & BITES

Introduction

I am delighted to introduce the *Irish Countrywomen's Association Book of Bread and Baking*. This is the fifth in the series of books written collectively by our members and this time we highlight bread recipes as well as cakes, biscuits and all manner of muffins and buns. We continue to receive very positive feedback from people in Ireland and all around the world who have used recipes from our first book, *The ICA Cookbook*; have cleaned their homes using homemade remedies from *The ICA Book of Home and Family*; enjoyed some of our reflections from *The ICA Book of Tea and Company*; or made a festive wreath from *The ICA Book of Christmas*.

We are very grateful to all of our members who have contributed to these five books over the last few years. They share their much-loved recipes, their thoughts, their inspirations and their top tips, many of which have been handed down through generations.

I have always been a keen baker, and have a particular love for freshly baked bread. I was lucky enough to grow up in a house where the smell of fresh bread was an integral part of home. Many supermarkets nowadays pump the aroma of baking around their stores to encourage you to buy their products. In my house, that smell encouraged you to spread a bit of home-churned butter and some delicious home-made jam on a warm slice before you ate it all up.

I have included in these pages a recipe for apple cake which is traditional to the area where I now live in Ardrahan, near Gort, Co. Galway. Of course, when I was growing up in Oldcastle, Co. Meath, my mother also made apple cakes, using apples from the local orchard for all of them. There are more than 70 varieties of heirloom apples grown in Ireland. They have very subtle differences of flavour as well as colour and texture. As our world becomes more globalised and homogenised it is possible to lose sight of the fact that local variations are what bring distinctive flavours to cooking as well as to life. We hope that in this book you will find recipes that celebrate these differences and highlight the distinct flavours, including everything from soda bread recipes that have been passed down through the generations to new recipes for gluten- and lactose-free breads.

Baking is an activity that you can enjoy with children from a young age and baking with my grandchildren is something that I love, even if it means a lot of mess in the kitchen afterwards. We in the ICA are very keen to preserve heritage and skills and pass them on to the next generations. We encourage you to take the time to enjoy the simple pleasures of baking an apple cake or a soda bread in the knowledge that generations have been using these recipes before you. Now that you have the book, you too can pass on this learning and heritage to the generations to come.

Josephine Helly
National President of the ICA

A NOTE FROM THE EDITOR, AOIFE CARRIGY

Who better than the women of the Irish Countrywomen's Association to share their much-loved bread and baking recipes passed down through generations?

As always in this series of recipes and recollections, the traditional stalwarts are well represented. You'll find within these pages several versions of traditional Irish soda bread alongside interesting twists on this national staple. There are fluffy scones, and a variety of fruit cakes to suit various palates. There's even a farmhouse country butter to spread on these simple delights.

There are timeless fruit-based cakes and puddings borne of the age-old shifts of seasonal abundance, from the first forced rhubarb through late summer's bountiful brambles and autumn's orchard fruits to the dried fruits and preserves that have brightened up many a dark Irish winter.

There are indulgences from more frugal times, when a simple chocolate cake was the mark of country house luxury or an apricot honey bread the height of globe-trotting exoticism. Some come from far and wide, picked up by young Irish women who had travelled across oceans to seek regular work and returned with new, treasured recipes to share with their families at home – and now shared here by their nieces, daughters or grand-daughters for future generations to enjoy.

Many of these recipes speak of particular moments in time: a 'Mystery Cake' devised of unlikely ingredients by resourceful American Depression-era bakers; an unforgettable upside-down treat etched on the memory of a five-year-old grandchild during the big snow of 1947. These sit shoulder-to-shoulder with recipes that appeal to our modern palates (sourdough breads, onion focaccia, chewy chocolate chip cookies) and contemporary dietary requirements (vegan blackberry cake and gluten-free breads).

Others tell the unspoken stories so often bound up in the sharing of recipes. These scribbled instructions or torn-out magazine pages become precious keepsakes that, in their recreation, allow for a reconnection with a remembered loved one: a son and his Parisian girlfriend living in Barcelona, for instance, or a friend's mother who acted in a small but significant moment of kindness. And many are rooted in very particular places, like the crumble cake inspired by the glorious mulberry trees in An Grianán or Josephine Helly's tribute to the place that she has made her home.

There is something for everyone here, from the simple to the show-stopping. There are wholesome seeded breads and gooey chocolate pudding; mocha muffins or bacon and peanut butter muffins; simple queen cakes and marmalade shortcakes alongside indulgent whiskey and salted caramel cake. There are quick and easy cakes to bake in a flash for unexpected visitors, others with which to while away a lazy day and some that require love and attention over several days or even weeks. Apart from a handful from ICA cookery tutors Janice Casey Bracken and Edward Hayden, all of these recipes have come from ICA members, been re-tested for this cookbook and in some cases tweaked very slightly to give you at home the best recipe for successful baking.

We hope that you enjoy the reading and learning, the baking and sharing and of course the eating!

KRUPS
MADE IN THE IRISH REPUBLIC

Chapter 1
Soda Breads

Simple Brown Bread

BER ENNIS, HORSELEAP STREAMSTOWN GUILD, WESTMEATH

I love baking and this recipe in particular has proved a real winner, having secured first prize at many local agricultural shows as well as representing Westmeath in the ICA Brown Bread competition.

Makes one large loaf

- 285g (10oz) self-raising flour, sieved
- 50g (2oz) wheat bran
- 50g (2oz) wholemeal flour
- 1 teaspoon salt
- ½ teaspoon bicarbonate of soda
- 50g (2oz) butter, melted
- 400ml (¾ pint) buttermilk
- 2 eggs, beaten

what you'll need

- 900g (2lb) loaf tin
- wire rack

1. Preheat oven to 200°C/400°F/Gas 6. Grease a 900g (2lb) loaf tin.
2. Combine all the dry ingredients in a large mixing bowl, stirring to mix well.
3. In a separate bowl, beat the melted butter and buttermilk into the eggs. Add to the dry ingredients, stirring to mix well into a wet dough.
4. Pour into the prepared loaf tin and bake in the preheated oven for 50–60 minutes or until the base sounds hollow when knocked.
5. Remove from the oven and turn out onto a wire rack to cool fully before slicing.

White Soda Bread

ANNETTE LONG, CASTLETROY GUILD, LIMERICK

This simple white soda bread is a useful staple to have in your repertoire. If you prefer a sweeter style of bread, you could add a handful or two of mixed dried fruit together with the sugar before baking.

Makes one large loaf

- 450g (1lb) plain flour
- 1 teaspoon bicarbonate of soda
- 1 teaspoon cream of tartar
- a pinch of salt
- 25g (1oz) butter or margarine
- 25g (1oz) caster sugar
- 330ml (11fl oz) buttermilk

what you'll need

- 900g (1lb) loaf tin or flat baking sheet
- wire rack

ICA Tip

Acidic cream of tartar (which is powdered tartaric acid) helps to activate the alkaline bicarbonate of soda in this recipe. You can substitute the teaspoon of tartar with two teaspoons of lemon juice instead, or substitute both the tartar and soda for two teaspoons of baking powder.

1. Preheat oven to 180°C/350°F/Gas 4. Grease a 900g (1lb) loaf tin, if using, or lightly flour a baking sheet.

2. Sieve the dry ingredients into a large mixing bowl and rub in the butter or margarine with your fingers until you have a crumb-like texture.

3. Add the sugar and buttermilk and mix to a soft dough.

4. Transfer to the greased loaf tin, if using. If using the baking sheet, place the dough on a floured surface, shape into a round cake, cut a cross on top and transfer to the floured sheet. Bake in the preheated oven for 45 minutes or until the base sounds hollow when knocked.

5. Remove from the oven and turn onto a wire rack to cool fully before slicing.

Wholemeal Soda Bread

BREDA MCDONALD, MULLINAVAT GUILD, KILKENNY

Breda McDonald was one of the stars of RTÉ's popular ICA Bootcamp *television series. She is well known for her traditional homemade country butter (see page 21), for which this delicious bread makes a wonderful backdrop.*

Makes one large loaf

- 350g (12oz) wholemeal flour
- 50g (2oz) porridge oats
- 50g (2oz) plain flour
- 2 level teaspoons bicarbonate of soda
- a pinch of salt
- 2 large eggs
- 1 tablespoon sunflower oil
- 500ml (17fl oz) buttermilk

to finish

- a handful of porridge oats

what you'll need

- 900g (2lb) loaf tin
- wire rack

ICA Tip

Traditional farmhouse country butter is becoming more widely available, especially in local farmers' markets or speciality food stores. We've included Breda's homemade butter recipe on page 21, if you feel up to the challenge of making your own.

1. Preheat oven to 170°C/325°F/Gas 3. Generously grease a 900g (2lb) loaf tin.
2. Combine the wholemeal flour and porridge oats in a large mixing bowl. Sieve in the plain flour, soda and salt, mix together and make a well in the centre.
3. In a separate bowl, beat the eggs together with the oil and add to the dry mixture. Mix in the buttermilk and combine well to create a sloppy consistency.
4. Pour into the prepared loaf tin and smooth the top with a wet spoon. Sprinkle the top of the bread with some additional oats.
5. Bake in the preheated oven for an hour, then remove the bread from the tin and return it to the oven shelf for a further 20 minutes or until the base sounds hollow when knocked.
6. Remove from the oven and turn out onto a wire rack to cool fully before slicing.

Cheddar and Spring Onion Bread

MARGARET O'GORMAN, CAMROSS GUILD, WEXFORD

This delicious savoury bread is my twist on a white soda loaf. Like most white soda breads, it is best eaten within a few hours so do make it on the day you plan to eat it. Toasting it will help give it fresh life later in the day.

Makes one round, crusty loaf

- 450g (1lb) plain flour
- 1 teaspoon bicarbonate of soda
- 1 teaspoon salt
- 100g (3½oz) Cheddar, grated
- 4 spring onions, trimmed and finely chopped
- 310–350ml (10½–11½ fl oz) buttermilk

what you'll need

- flat baking sheet
- wire rack

1. Preheat oven to 220°C/425°F/Gas 7. Lightly flour a baking sheet.

2. Sieve the flour, soda and salt into a large mixing bowl. Mix in the cheese and spring onions.

3. Make a well in the centre of the dry ingredients. Add about 300ml (10fl oz) of the buttermilk, and use a wooden spoon to mix gently and quickly until you have a nice soft dough, adding more buttermilk little by little, if necessary, to bind the dough together but without letting it get sloppy.

4. Turn onto a floured surface and knead very lightly before shaping into a round of about 15cm (6in) in diameter. Place on the baking sheet and cut a deep cross in the top.

5. Bake in the preheated oven for 15 minutes, then reduce the temperature to 200°C/400°F/Gas 6 and bake for another 20–25 minutes or until the base sounds hollow when knocked and the top is golden all over. Remove from the oven and leave on a wire rack to cool.

Honey-Nut Brown Bread

JOAN HAYES, CRECORA GUILD, LIMERICK

The following is a recipe I use all the time and is loved by family and friends alike. It's a nice twist on a traditional brown soda bread, but with lots of wholesome nuts and seeds added.

Makes one large loaf

- 450g (1lb) brown flour
- 1 heaped teaspoon bicarbonate of soda
- 110g (4oz) butter, cubed
- 110g (4oz) walnuts, whole or crumbled slightly
- 110g (4oz) sunflower seeds
- 110g (4oz) pumpkin seeds
- 25g (1oz) golden linseed
- 1 egg
- 2 tablespoons honey
- 325–375ml (11–12fl oz) buttermilk

what you'll need

- 900g (2lb) loaf tin
- wire rack

ICA Tip

You could remove the bread from its tin and return to the oven for the last 10 minutes of baking if you prefer a crispier crust.

1. Preheat oven to 180°C/350°F/Gas 4. Grease a 900g (2lb) loaf tin.

2. Put the flour in a large mixing bowl, sieve in the soda then rub in the butter with your fingers until you have a crumb-like texture. Mix in the remaining dry ingredients and make a well in the centre.

3. In a separate bowl, beat the egg and add to the dry mixture together with the honey and most of the buttermilk. Mix well, either with wet hands or a wooden spoon; it should form a sloppy dough, but you can add more buttermilk if necessary.

4. Transfer to the prepared loaf tin and bake in the preheated oven for about 70–80 minutes or until the base sounds hollow when knocked.

5. Remove from the oven and turn onto a wire rack to cool. This will keep very well for a few days, but also freezes very well (slice first for convenience).

Lactose-Free Brown Bread

RITA ALVES, DROGHEDA GUILD, LOUTH

Despite being lactose intolerant, one of my favourite Irish treats has always been a breakfast with homemade brown soda bread made with buttermilk. The best version I ever tasted was made by Mary Bailey, my husband's aunt, who very kindly shared her famous (and generally well-kept) recipe, which I adapted to create my own lactose-free recipe. It won a prize at the National Brown Bread Baking Competition at the National Ploughing Championships in 2017.

Makes one large loaf

- 500ml (17fl oz) lactose-free milk (e.g. Avonmore Lactose-Free Milk)
- 3 tablespoons lemon juice
- 285g (10oz) wholemeal flour
- 1½ teaspoons bicarbonate of soda
- 1 teaspoon salt
- 170g (6oz) plain flour
- 25g (1oz) plant-based margarine
- 5 tablespoons oats
- 2 tablespoons sunflower seeds, some reserved to sprinkle over the top
- 1 tablespoon Demerara sugar
- 1 egg

what you'll need

- 900g (2lb) loaf tin
- baking parchment
- palette knife or spatula
- wire rack

1. Mix the lactose-free milk and lemon juice in a bowl or jug and set aside for about 10 minutes to curdle.
2. Preheat oven to 200°C/400°F/Gas 6. Grease a 900g (2lb) loaf tin and line the base with baking parchment.
3. In a large mixing bowl, combine the wholemeal flour, soda and salt and sieve in the plain flour. Add the margarine and then rub in with your fingers until you have a crumb-like texture. Mix in the oats, sunflower seeds and sugar.
4. Beat the egg with the curdled milk, then gradually work the mixture into the dry ingredients, incorporating each addition before adding the next.
5. Transfer the mixture to the prepared baking tin, smooth over the top with a palette knife or spatula and sprinkle with sunflower seeds. Run a sharp knife lengthways down the middle of the bread about 2.5cm (1in) deep and put it straight into the preheated oven.
6. Reduce the oven temperature to 190°C/375°F/Gas 5 and bake for 45–55 minutes or until the base sounds hollow when knocked. Remove from the oven and turn out onto a wire rack to cool fully.

ICA Tip

Lactose-free milk is cow's milk with the addition of an enzyme called lactase, which breaks down the lactose and makes the milk easier to digest. It retains the flavour and nutritional benefits of regular cow's milk.

Rich Brown Bread

MARGARET O'HARA, BONNICONLON GUILD, MAYO

This is the recipe I used when I represented Mayo Federation in the Aldi Brown Bread Competition in An Grianán in August 2015, which was a great experience. I have also won the ICA Brown Bread Competition at our local show with this recipe. The addition of wheat bran, wheat germ and nuts really add something to the texture, while the inclusion of cream and honey enrich the final flavour.

Makes one large loaf

- 350g (12oz) wholemeal flour
- 50g (2oz) porridge oats, plus extra for sprinkling
- 50g (2oz) wheat bran
- 50g (2oz) wheat germ
- 50g (2oz) plain flour
- 2 teaspoons bicarbonate of soda
- a pinch of salt
- 50g (2oz) butter, cubed
- 50g (2oz) flaked almonds
- 50g (2oz) walnuts
- 2 large eggs
- 2 tablespoons honey
- 60ml (2fl oz) double cream
- 570ml (1 pint) buttermilk
- 2 tablespoons sesame seeds

what you'll need

- 900g (2lb) loaf tin
- wire rack

1. Preheat oven to 170°C/325°F/Gas 3. Grease a 900g (2lb) loaf tin.

2. Mix the wholemeal flour, porridge oats, wheat bran and wheat germ in a large mixing bowl, sieve in the plain flour, soda and salt and mix well.

3. Rub in the butter with your fingers until you have a crumb-like texture. Add the flaked almonds and walnuts, mix together and make a well in the centre.

4. In a separate bowl, beat the eggs, add the honey, cream and buttermilk and mix together. Add this to the dry mixture and combine well until it reaches a sloppy consistency.

5. Pour into the prepared loaf tin and smooth the top of the dough with a wet spoon. Sprinkle over the sesame seeds and some additional oats.

6. Bake in the preheated oven for 80 minutes or until the base sounds hollow when knocked. Remove from the oven and allow to cool on a wire rack before slicing.

ICA Tip

Some bakers recommend removing the bread from the tin for the last 20 minutes of baking in order to crisp up the crust nicely.

Savoury Soda Bread

EILISH MCDONNELL, HORSELEAP STREAMSTOWN GUILD, WESTMEATH

I created this savoury bread recipe for my daughter Caroline, who is vegetarian. It is based on my prize-winning white soda bread, which my grandchildren love fried with butter on the pan when they call on cold Saturday mornings! It's delicious served with salads.

Makes one large pizza-style loaf

- 450g (1lb) plain flour
- ½ teaspoon bicarbonate of soda
- a pinch of salt
- 330ml (11fl oz) buttermilk
- 2–3 tablespoons good-quality pesto
- 1 red onion, peeled and finely sliced
- 1 red pepper, cored, de-seeded and sliced
- 1 tablespoon olive oil
- salt and freshly ground black pepper

what you'll need

- baking sheet or tray
- wire rack

ICA *Tip*

The secret to a good white soda bread is to mix it quickly and not overwork the dough. It should feel light when it is going into the oven.

1. Preheat oven to 200°C/400°F/Gas 6. Lightly flour a baking sheet or tray.

2. Sieve the flour, soda and salt into a large mixing bowl. Add most of the buttermilk and quickly mix it together into a light dough, adding more if needed.

3. Turn out onto a lightly floured surface and knead it two or three times, then press it out flat to about 1cm (½in) thick.

4. Spread the pesto over the dough, then arrange the slices of red onion and red pepper on top, pressing these into the dough. Drizzle with olive oil and season with salt and pepper.

5. Transfer carefully to the floured baking sheet. Bake in the preheated for about 40–50 minutes or until the base sounds hollow when knocked. The cooked bread should feel light.

6. Remove from the oven and allow to cool a little on a wire rack before slicing. Serve hot or cold.

Spelt Soda Bread

HELEN CRONOGUE, ANNADUFF GUILD, LEITRIM

This simple soda bread recipe replaces regular wheat flour with spelt flour, which is made from an ancient form of wheat that is much lower in gluten than modern forms of wheat. Spelt is not gluten-free, however, and is not suitable for coeliacs, but some people who report a sensitivity to gluten find it easier to digest.

Makes one large loaf

- 340g (12oz) white spelt flour
- 1 teaspoon bicarbonate of soda
- ½ teaspoon salt
- 110g (4oz) wholemeal spelt flour
- 400ml (¾ pint) buttermilk
- 1 tablespoon olive oil

to finish (optional)

- 2 tablespoons sesame seeds

what you'll need

- 900g (2lb) loaf tin
- baking parchment
- wire rack

1. Preheat oven to 220°C/425°F/Gas 7. Grease a 900g (2lb) loaf tin and line with baking parchment.

2. Sieve the white spelt flour and soda into a large mixing bowl, add the salt and wholemeal spelt flour, and mix well.

3. Make a well in the centre of the flour mixture and pour in the buttermilk and olive oil together. Using your hands or a wooden spoon, combine all the ingredients into a wet dough.

4. Transfer the mixture into the prepared loaf tin and sprinkle with the sesame seeds, if using. Run a knife about 2.5cm (1in) deep lengthways down the centre of the bread, to help it rise evenly and release air in the centre rather than to one side.

5. Bake in the preheated oven for about 40–50 minutes or until the base sounds hollow when knocked. Remove from the oven and turn out onto a wire rack to cool fully before slicing.

Sun-Dried Tomato and Pesto Bread

RITA CAROLAN, CLONES GUILD, MONAGHAN

A family friend recently shared this recipe with me and it's quickly becoming a favourite among my friends and family. It's lovely to serve with homemade soup or simply straight out of the oven, smothered with butter.

Makes one medium loaf

- 450g (1lb) plain flour, plus extra for dusting
- 1 heaped teaspoon bicarbonate of soda
- ½ teaspoon salt
- 85g (3oz) sun-dried or semi-dried tomatoes, in oil
- 300ml (10fl oz) buttermilk
- 2 tablespoons basil pesto
- 50g (2oz) Parmesan cheese, grated

what you'll need

- baking sheet
- rolling pin
- wire rack

ICA Tip

This would work just as well with Irish wild garlic pesto if you want to celebrate the seasons and use some local produce.

1. Preheat oven to 180°C/350°F/Gas 4. Grease and flour a baking sheet.

2. Sieve the flour, soda and salt into a large mixing bowl.

3. Remove the tomatoes from their oil and pat dry with kitchen paper. Chop roughly and mix into the bowl of flour. Add enough buttermilk to make a soft dough, taking care not to make it too wet – you may only need about three-quarters of what you have.

4. Turn the dough onto a floured worktop and use a rolling pin to roll gently into a square of about 30cm (12in). Spread with the pesto and sprinkle over the grated cheese. Roll the dough up like a Swiss roll and transfer to the floured baking sheet. Dust the top with flour.

5. Bake in the preheated oven for about 45–50 minutes until golden brown. Transfer to a wire rack to cool a little before serving.

How to make ...

Homemade Farmhouse Country Butter

BREDA MCDONALD, MULLINAVAT GUILD, KILKENNY

A champion butter-maker, Breda was one of the mentors on RTÉ's ICA Bootcamp television series where she shared some of the many skills acquired through years of active membership in the ICA. This is her recipe for homemade butter.

- 1 litre (1¾ pints) cream for every 450g (1lb) butter
- salt, to taste

what you'll need

- glass churn, preferably (or plastic churn or stand mixer)
- Scotch hands/butter spades/paddles
- chopping board
- sieve
- butter stamps (optional)

ICA *Tip*

You can flavour homemade butter – or indeed any butter – with all sorts of ingredients, from chopped chives or wild garlic to orange zest or marmalade or even whiskey or brandy.

1. Sterilise your equipment meticulously. Scald the churner or stand mixer with boiling water, rinse with cold water and dry thoroughly.

2. Chill the cream to about 7°C (45°F) to help the buttermilk to separate from the solids. The better they separate, the longer the shelf life of the butter.

3. Put the chilled cream into the glass churning jar. Do not fill more than one third full.

4. Churn gently for 10–15 minutes. When the churn handle becomes harder to turn, this indicates that the butter is leaving the buttermilk. When the butter is churned correctly, it will be the size of wheat grains. If using a mixer, beat slowly and take care not to mix the buttermilk back into the butter.

5. Strain off the buttermilk and reserve it for making brown or white soda bread. Add some chilled water and wash the butter until the water is clean; this will take at least three rinses with fresh water. Strain the reserved butter into a sieve and allow the excess water to drain off it completely.

6. Transfer the butter to a chopping board and season with a little salt, according to your preferences. Beat with Scotch hands, spades or butter paddles to ensure the salt is well distributed and to knock out any excess moisture. Mould into the desired shape and stamp with butter stamps, if using, to get a nice imprint on the top.

7. Wrap in greaseproof paper or baking parchment and refrigerate for up to one month.

Chapter 2
Sweetened Breads, Fruit Cakes & Brack

Apricot Honey Bread

MARGARET FERGUSON, HORACE PLUNKETT/DUNSANY GUILD, MEATH

Growing up on a farm in West Clare in the 1950s, I had an aunt who lived in the States who we didn't see very often but my mother spoke about her regularly. She was a wonderful cook and worked for a very wealthy family. When she finally came home to visit us, it caused quite a stir in our house. We were so excited to see her and boy did she live up to our expectations! She introduced us to some very exotic ingredients such as coffee, vanilla and apricots. We used the apricots and nuts that came from the States and the honey that came from our own bee hives to bake this bread together and it was absolutely divine. I will never forget that taste! I am certain that this was the seed that grew into my lifelong love for cooking.

Makes one medium loaf

- 85g (3oz) dried apricots
- 170g (6oz) plain flour
- 2 teaspoons baking powder
- 1 teaspoon salt
- 50g (2oz) caster sugar
- 50g (2oz) butter
- 150ml (¼ pint) milk
- 4 tablespoons (170g/6oz) honey
- 1 egg, beaten
- 50g (2oz) nuts (such as walnuts, almonds or pecans), finely chopped

what you'll need

- 900g (2lb) loaf tin
- wire rack

ICA Tip

Dried apricots are preserved with sulphur dioxide to prevent the fruit oxidising and turning brown. Alternatively, naturally dried apricots from the health food shop will have a darker colour but the same flavour.

1. Preheat oven to 180°C/350°F/Gas 4. Grease a 900g (2lb) loaf tin and line with baking parchment.
2. Soak the apricots in a little boiling water and set aside until cool.
3. Sieve the flour, baking powder and salt together into a large mixing bowl and mix in the sugar. Melt the butter in a small pan, cool slightly then stir in the milk, honey and beaten egg. Add this mixture into the bowl of flour and stir.
4. Drain and finely chop the apricots and mix into the batter, together with the nuts.
5. Spoon the batter into the prepared tin and allow to stand for about 20 minutes.
6. Bake in the preheated oven for about 50–60 minutes, or until it is golden brown all over and the base sounds hollow when knocked.
7. Remove from the oven and leave in the tin to cool for a few minutes before turning out onto a wire rack. Serve warm or cold.

Pumpkin Bread

MARIE MCCORMACK, COLLINSTOWN/FORE GUILD, WESTMEATH

This sweet, moist bread is as easy to bake as it is delicious to eat. The only challenge might be in finding tinned pumpkin, or fresh pumpkins in season, but you could replace the pumpkin with butternut squash, which is from the same family and widely available for much of the year.

Makes one large loaf

- 1 medium pumpkin/ butternut squash or 175g (6oz) pumpkin purée (use a tinned brand like Libby's)
- 250g (9oz) plain flour
- 1 teaspoon baking powder
- 1 teaspoon bicarbonate of soda
- 1 teaspoon ground cinnamon
- 175g (6oz) caster sugar
- 100ml (3½fl oz) vegetable oil
- 2 eggs
- 110g (4oz) raisins

what you'll need

- 2lb (900g) loaf tin

ICA *Tip*

You could also peel, deseed and cube the pumpkin flesh and cook in simmering water for about 20 minutes before puréeing, but the results may contain a higher water content than the roasted alternative. Freshly cooked pumpkin purée will keep well for up to three days in the fridge or three months in the freezer.

1. Preheat oven to 180°C/350°F/Gas 4. Grease a 2lb (900g) loaf tin with oil.

2. If you can't find tinned pumpkin, you can roast a fresh pumpkin or butternut squash and purée its flesh. Simply halve the pumpkin lengthways, scoop out the seeds and surrounding membrane, drizzle the flesh with a little oil and roast in the preheated oven for about 45 minutes. Allow to cool, scoop out the cooked flesh and blitz or mash to a purée.

3. Sieve the flour, baking powder, soda and cinnamon into a mixing bowl.

4. Combine the sugar and oil in another large mixing bowl and mix well. Beat the first egg and mix it in, incorporating fully before repeating with the second egg.

5. Fold the dry ingredients into the wet a quarter at a time, and then add the pumpkin purée and raisins.

6. Transfer to the prepared loaf tin. Bake in the preheated oven for one hour or until a skewer inserted into the centre comes out clean.

7. Remove from the oven and allow to cool in the tin for a few minutes before transferring to a wire rack to cool fully.

Gingerbread

BRIDGET O'MALLEY, ARDMORE/GRANGE GUILD, WATERFORD

This gorgeous recipe offers all you want in a gingerbread: a soft moreish texture but with crispy edges for contrast, layers of dark sweet flavours thanks to its combination of sugar, syrup and treacle and the warming heat of ginger bringing the whole thing together. The only thing that can improve it is mountains of salted Irish butter and a pot of hot tea.

Serves 8

- 150ml (¼ pint) milk
- 110g (4oz) margarine
- 110g (4oz) brown sugar
- 110g (4oz) golden syrup
- 110g (4oz) treacle
- ½ level teaspoon bicarbonate of soda
- 225g (8oz) plain flour
- 3–4 level teaspoons ground ginger
- 1 egg, beaten

what you'll need

- deep 18cm (7in) square tin
- baking parchment
- wire rack

1. Preheat oven to 180°C/350°F/Gas 4. Grease a deep 18cm (7in) square tin and line with baking parchment.

2. In a medium saucepan, combine the milk, margarine, sugar, syrup and treacle and stir over a low heat for about 10 minutes or until the margarine has melted and the sugar has dissolved. Remove from the heat and sieve in the soda, which will fizz a little. Mix thoroughly to ensure the soda is fully incorporated and set aside to cool to body temperature (approx. 36°C).

3. Sieve the flour and ginger into a large mixing bowl and make a well in the centre. Once the milk and soda mixture has cooled sufficiently, stir in the beaten egg (doing this while the mixture is hot might make the egg scramble). Pour this into the bowl of dry ingredients, mix together and beat until smooth.

4. Pour into the prepared cake tin and bake on the middle shelf of the preheated oven for 55–65 minutes or until a skewer inserted into the centre comes out clean.

5. Leave in the tin for a few minutes before turning out, removing the paper and leaving to cool fully on a wire rack. Store in an airtight container where it will keep well and improve in flavour over the following days.

Spicy Banana Bread

MAURA WALSH, CAPPAMORE GUILD, LIMERICK

This moist and tasty recipe is a firm favourite in our house, and usually disappears pretty quickly! Part of the beauty of it is that it uses up ripe bananas that otherwise may be in danger of being consigned to the bin. It is also 'healthy' in that bananas are a good source of potassium. Most important, it's delicious.

Makes one large loaf

- 110g (4oz) butter, softened
- 110g (4oz) caster sugar
- 2 eggs, beaten
- 4 over-ripe bananas, 3 mashed and 1 chopped
- 225g (8oz) self-raising flour
- 1 teaspoon baking powder
- 1 teaspoon ground mixed spice
- 1 teaspoon ground cinnamon
- ½ teaspoon ground ginger
- 175g (6oz) mixed dried fruit

what you'll need

- 900g (2lb) loaf tin
- baking parchment
- wire rack

1. Preheat oven to 180°C/350°F/Gas 4. Grease a 900g (2lb) loaf tin and line with parchment.
2. Cream together the butter and sugar in a large mixing bowl, then add the beaten eggs. Add the mashed and chopped banana to the mixture and stir to mix.
3. Sieve and fold in the flour together with the baking powder and spices, then fold in the dried fruit.
4. Transfer to the prepared loaf tin and bake in the preheated oven until a skewer inserted into the centre comes out clean, which will be anywhere between 45 and 60 minutes depending on the size of your bananas.
5. Allow to cool slightly before turning out onto a wire rack to cool completely. This very moist recipe is best eaten fresh, but can be wrapped in parchment and tinfoil and stored in an airtight container for a few days.

ICA *Tip*

To speed up the ripening of bananas, store them in a warm place, such as a hot press, inside a brown paper bag to trap the ethylene (a gaseous plant hormone that bananas emit naturally). Popping them (unpeeled) in the oven as it preheats will also help to sweeten them further.

Treacle and Raisin Bread

SHEILA BAYNES, CASTLEBAR GUILD, MAYO

My late mother used to bake homemade bread in a pot oven on the hearth. She never weighed anything; instead ingredients were measured in fists of this or that and pinches of the lesser ingredients. During the late 1940s and early 1950s, when Ireland was recovering from the after-effects of the Second World War, ration books were still in operation and were very valuable. Every autumn a parcel would arrive from America with spices and large Californian raisins (to be cut small) which we could bake into treats like this delicious treacle bread.

Serves 12

- 675g (1½lb) plain flour
- 2 teaspoons bicarbonate of soda
- 2 teaspoons ground ginger
- 1 teaspoon mixed spice
- a pinch of salt
- 110g (4oz) margarine
- 175g (6oz) caster sugar
- 175g (6oz) raisins
- 400ml (¾ pint) buttermilk or sour milk
- 3 tablespoons treacle
- 2 large eggs, beaten

what you'll need

- round 23cm (9in) baking tin
- baking parchment
- wire rack

1. Preheat oven to 180°C/350°F/Gas 4. Grease and line a round 23cm (9in) baking tin with baking parchment.

2. Sieve the flour, soda, spices and salt into a large mixing bowl and rub in the margarine with your fingers until you have a crumb-like texture. Add the sugar and raisins and mix well.

3. Gently heat a little of the milk in a saucepan with the treacle, or alternatively loosen the treacle by warming in the microwave for no longer than 15 seconds. Beat the eggs in a mixing bowl, add the remaining milk and the loosened treacle and mix well.

4. Add the wet ingredients to the flour mixture and stir well to bring together into a wet dough. Transfer the mixture into the lined baking tin.

5. Bake in the preheated oven for about 90 minutes or until the bread is browned all over and a skewer inserted into the centre comes out clean.

6. Remove from the oven and leave in the tin to cool for a few minutes before turning out onto a wire rack to cool fully.

LACK TREACLE
LYLE & SONS
SUGAR REFINERS
454g e

Boiled Guinness Cake

PATTY O'BRIEN, ABBEYKNOCKMOY GUILD, GALWAY

This is a versatile cake that can be baked into a cake or a loaf, or as a couple of small loaves, which make handy gifts when visiting a friend. You can replace the Guinness with equal quantities of tea to make a boiled fruit cake.

Serves 12

- 275ml (½ pint) Guinness from a bottle or can
- 225g (8oz) butter
- 225g (8oz) soft brown sugar
- 225g (8oz) raisins
- 225g (8oz) sultanas
- 110g (4oz) dried cherries
- 50g (2oz) mixed peel
- 1 rounded teaspoon bicarbonate of soda
- 570g (1lb 4oz) plain flour
- 1 rounded teaspoon mixed spice
- 1 rounded teaspoon ground nutmeg
- 50g (2oz) ground almonds
- 3 eggs, well beaten

what you'll need

- spatula or palette knife
- 1 x deep 20cm (8in) cake tin
  or
  2 x 900g (2lb) loaf tins
  or
  4 x 450g (1lb) loaf tins
- baking parchment
- tinfoil
- wire rack

1. Preheat oven to 170°C/325°F/Gas 3. Grease the tin(s) and line the base(s) with baking parchment.

2. Combine the Guinness, butter and sugar in a large saucepan, bring to the boil and simmer, stirring, until the butter is melted and the sugar completely dissolved. Add the dried fruit and mixed peel and simmer over a low heat for another four or five minutes.

3. Remove from heat, add the soda and mix well before setting aside to cool. (If you want to speed up the cooling, you can fill the sink with cold water and partly submerge the saucepan in it, stirring to help the cooling process.)

4. Meanwhile, sieve the flour and spices into a large mixing bowl and add the ground almonds.

5. Add the beaten eggs to the cooled Guinness mixture, mixing well. Add the sieved ingredients and stir together, mixing until you have a slow dropping consistency. Turn into the prepared tin(s) and smooth the top with a spatula or palette knife.

6. Bake on the middle shelf of the preheated oven for about 90 minutes if using one deep 20cm (8in) cake tin. Alternatively, bake for about 75 minutes for 900g (2lb) loaf tins, or about 60 minutes for 450g (1lb) loaf tins. Whichever size you are using, check the cake after an hour; it is ready when a skewer inserted into the centre comes out clean.

7. Remove from the oven and leave in the tin on a wire rack to cool fully before removing baking parchment. Wrap in fresh parchment and then tinfoil and store in an airtight container, where it will keep for at least a week. If you can resist cutting for a few days, the flavour will improve in that time.

Mixed Fruit Soda Bread

PAULINE MCENERNEY, CROSSERLOUGH GUILD, CAVAN

This recipe comes from my mother, Bridget Fahy, and I still have it in her handwriting. I believe she would have used it in the late 1940s and in the 1950s. The cake was made after the Second World War when there was little butter and very few eggs. Nowadays, however, it's particularly nice served slathered with lots of butter!

Serves 12

- 450g (1lb) plain flour
- ½ teaspoon grated nutmeg
- a pinch of salt
- 110g (4oz) butter, cubed
- 85g (3oz) lard or vegetable shortening (e.g. Cookeen)
- 225g (8oz) brown sugar
- 225g (8oz) sultanas
- 225g (8oz) currants
- 110g (4oz) mixed peel
- 1 teaspoon bicarbonate of soda
- 300ml (10fl oz) milk
- 2 teaspoons distilled vinegar

what you'll need

- 20cm (8in) round baking tin
- baking parchment
- wire rack

1. Preheat oven to 180°C/350°F/Gas 4. Grease a 20cm (8in) round baking tin and line with baking parchment.

2. Sieve the flour, nutmeg and salt into a large mixing bowl. Rub in the butter and shortening with your fingers until you have a crumb-like texture. Stir in the sugar, dried fruit and mixed peel.

3. Dissolve the soda in a little milk, and then stir this together with the rest of the milk into the dry ingredients, mixing lightly before adding the vinegar. Mix well to incorporate evenly.

4. Transfer the mixture to the prepared tin and bake in preheated oven for 1½–2 hours or until a skewer inserted into the centre comes out clean.

5. Remove from the oven and leave on a wire rack to cool before removing from the tin.

Our Spotted Dick

BETTY GORMAN, CASTLETOWN GUILD, LAOIS

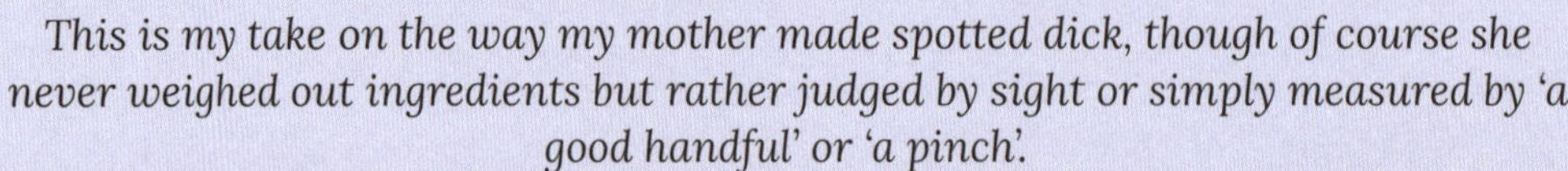

This is my take on the way my mother made spotted dick, though of course she never weighed out ingredients but rather judged by sight or simply measured by 'a good handful' or 'a pinch'.

Makes one round loaf

- 450g (1lb) plain flour
- 1 teaspoon bicarbonate of soda
- 1 teaspoon salt
- 110g (4oz) mixed dried fruit
- 50g (2oz) caster sugar
- 400ml (¾ pint) buttermilk

what you'll need

- baking sheet
- clean tea towel
- wire rack

ICA Tip

The classic spotted dick is a soft steamed pudding, but in Ireland it is typically baked and more like a fruity white soda bread. If you prefer a harder crust, don't cover with a tea towel while cooling.

1. Preheat oven to 200°C/400°F/Gas 6. Lightly flour a baking sheet.
2. Sieve the flour, soda and salt into a large mixing bowl. Add the dried fruit and sugar and mix well.
3. Make a well in the centre, and add enough of the buttermilk to bring together into a soft dough.
4. Turn onto a lightly floured board or worktop and shape into a circle. Cut a cross in the centre of the bread and transfer to the floured baking sheet.
5. Bake in the preheated oven for about 45 minutes or until the base sounds hollow when knocked and the top is golden all over.
6. Remove from the oven, cover with a clean tea towel and leave on a wire rack to cool for 20 minutes before serving warm or cold. This will last for a couple of days, stored in brown paper or parchment, and is delicious toasted and buttered.

Porter Cake

ANNE MARIA DENNISON, MAINISTIR NA FÉILE GUILD, LIMERICK

This is my favourite porter cake. It is easy to make using the rubbing-in method. I like to add a few quartered cherries and to soak the mixed fruit overnight in spirits for extra flavour (although this step is not essential if you don't have the time). I make some extra cakes at Christmas time to give as presents.

Serves 12

- 900g (2lb) mixed dried fruit (including optional cherries)
- 2 tablespoons whiskey or orange juice (optional, see method)
- 450g (1lb) self-raising flour
- 1½ teaspoons mixed spice
- 1 teaspoon baking powder
- 225g (8oz) butter, cubed
- 225g (8oz) brown sugar
- 2 eggs
- 250ml (8fl oz) stout
- 2 teaspoons treacle

what you'll need

- 20cm (8in) round cake tin
- greaseproof paper or baking parchment
- brown paper
- twine
- spatula or palette knife
- wire rack
- tinfoil

ICA Tip

As ovens may vary be prepared to adjust the baking temperature and baking time.

1. The mixed fruit can be plumped up by heating in a microwave for one minute, before soaking overnight in the whiskey or orange juice, if using, although this step is optional.

2. Preheat oven to 180°C/350°F/Gas 4. Line the base and sides of a 20cm (8in) round cake tin with greaseproof paper. Wrap the outside of the tin with brown paper (or a double layer of parchment) to a height of least 7½cm (3in) above the top of the tin. Secure with twine.

3. Sieve the flour, mixed spice and baking powder into a large mixing bowl. Rub in the butter in with your fingers until completely combined into a crumb-like texture. Mix in the brown sugar and mixed fruit.

4. Beat the eggs in a small bowl and add the stout. Make a well in the centre of the dry ingredients, pour in this egg-stout mixture together with the treacle, and mix with a wooden spoon until well combined. Transfer to the prepared baking tin and smooth out the top with a spatula or palette knife.

5. Bake in the centre of the preheated oven for an hour, then cover with greaseproof paper and lower the heat to 170°C/325°F/Gas 3. Continue to bake for about another hour or until a skewer inserted into the centre comes out clean.

6. Remove from the oven and leave in the tin on a wire rack to cool fully. Turn out and wrap in greaseproof paper and then tinfoil, and store in an airtight container for a few days before cutting (this will improve the flavour). It can then be cut into quarters, re-wrapped and stored in an airtight container, where it will keep well for a few weeks. It also freezes well.

Oxford Lunch

CAROLINE POWER, RATOATH GUILD, MEATH

When myself and my sisters first got married and set up our own homes, we gathered our grandmother's and mother's recipes together into little recipe books for ourselves. My copy is now well-battered through use, and to this day we still regularly use our grandmother's Christmas cake and pudding recipes. I adapted this one for a Gem Pack baking competition. Granny always baked in a range, so it took some tweaking to get the conditions correct for a good bake in a modern oven, but I am delighted I persisted. I had forgotten how versatile the Oxford lunch is and it was lovely to be using my grandmother's recipes again.

Makes one square fruit cake or two low loaves

- 240g (8½oz) margarine
- 225g (8oz) caster sugar
- 250g (9oz) plain flour
- 65g (2½oz) self-raising flour
- 5 eggs, beaten
- 675g (1½lb) sultanas
- 340g (12oz) raisins
- 50g (2oz) mixed peel
- 50g (2oz) glacé cherries
- 3 drops vanilla extract
- 2 drops almond extract

what you'll need

- 23cm (9in) square tin or 2 x 900g (2lb) loaf tins
- baking parchment
- stand mixer
- spatula
- tinfoil

1. Preheat oven to 140°C/275°F/Gas 1. Grease a 23cm (9in) square tin or two 900g (2lb) loaf tins and line with baking parchment.

2. Cream the margarine and sugar together using a stand mixer until pale, light and fluffy. Sieve the plain flour and self-raising flour together into a separate bowl.

3. Add about a third of the beaten egg to the margarine and sugar mixture and mix until well incorporated. Add about a third of the sieved flours and mix well. Repeat with the remaining egg and flour alternately, mixing each well before adding the next addition.

4. Fold in the dried fruit, peel, cherries and flavouring extracts using a wooden spoon, stirring from the bottom to incorporate evenly through the thick and lumpy batter.

5. Transfer to the prepared tin, or divide the mixture between two tins, if using, and smooth the top with a spatula. Bake in the preheated oven for 75–85 minutes until light golden all over.

6. Remove from the oven and allow to cool in the tin before turning out. Wrap in greaseproof paper and then foil and store in an airtight container where it will keep well for up to a week.

Rich Christmas Cake

MARY FERGUS, BALLISODARE GUILD, SLIGO

I first made this cake way back in the 1960s and for many years after that. Traditionally, Christmas cake would be made in Irish households at some point in November, allowing at least three weeks for the cake to mature, with weekly feeds of alcohol to keep everything nice and moist.

Serves 10–12

- 225g (8oz) seedless muscatel raisins
- 225g (8oz) sultanas
- 225g (8oz) raisins
- 110g (4oz) mixed peel
- 50g (2oz) dried cherries
- 50g (2oz) blanched almonds (or whole almonds, see method)
- 50g (2oz) ground almonds
- grated rind of 1 orange, plus a little juice
- grated rind of 1 lemon, plus a little juice
- 1 medium apple, peeled and cored
- a few drops of vanilla extract
- a few drops of almond extract
- 5 eggs, beaten
- 225g (8oz) softened butter
- 225g (8oz) dark soft brown sugar
- ½ teaspoon mixed spice
- ½ teaspoon ground ginger
- ½ teaspoon ground cinnamon

[*continued over-page*]

1. Prepare all the fruit the night before baking: weigh out the dried fruit and whole and ground nuts into one bowl, and grate the citrus rind into another. Stir about two teaspoons each of lemon and orange juice into the grated rind, then grate in the apple and mix well. If you don't have blanched almonds, simply immerse whole almonds in boiling water for about five minutes and then squeeze each individually: the nut should slip out of its skin easily.

2. In a small bowl, beat the vanilla and almond extracts into the eggs. Cream the butter and sugar together in a large mixing bowl until light and fluffy. Add all the spices and mix well.

3. Add about a third of the egg mixture to the butter-sugar mixture and beat thoroughly. Sieve in about a third of the flour, and beat to incorporate, then repeat twice with the remaining egg and flour.

4. Stir in the grated citrus and apple mixture, followed by about two teaspoons each of rum and brandy. Gradually add the mixed dried fruit and nuts, mixing well before adding the next addition. Cover and leave overnight.

5. The next day, preheat oven to 170°C/325°F/Gas 3. Generously grease a 23cm (9in) round tin and line the base and inside walls with a double layer of baking parchment or greaseproof paper. Line the outside of the tin (base and side walls) with brown paper, tied in place with twine. Cut out a 23cm (9in) paper lid (brown, greaseproof or parchment) for the top of the cake.

- - →

- ¼ teaspoon grated nutmeg
- 350g (12oz) plain flour
- 50ml (2fl oz) rum
- 40ml (1½fl oz) brandy
- 1 tablespoon (15ml/½fl oz) sour milk or buttermilk (or regular milk soured with a squeeze of lemon)
- ½ teaspoon bicarbonate of soda

to finish (optional)

- 900g (2lb) marzipan, shop-bought or homemade (see tip)
- 5 egg whites
- 600g (1lb 5oz) icing sugar
- 1½ teaspoons glycerine

what you'll need

- 23cm (9in) round tin
- baking parchment or greaseproof paper
- brown paper
- twine
- tinfoil
- rolling pin (optional)
- electric whisk (optional, but recommended)

ICA Tip

To make your own marzipan, mix together 450g (1lb) each of ground almonds and icing sugar with two beaten eggs and a squeeze of lemon juice. You can use some warmed and loosened apricot jam or marmalade in place of the egg white to help the marzipan adhere to the cake.

6. Re-mix the cake mixture thoroughly and add about 20ml each of brandy and rum. Mix the sour milk (or buttermilk, if using) and soda in a small bowl before adding to the mixture and stirring well.

7. Transfer to the prepared tin and bake on the middle shelf of the preheated oven for 90 minutes, topping the cake halfway through with the prepared paper lid to stop it browning too quickly. Reduce the oven temperature to 150°C/300°F/Gas 2 for another 2–2½ hours or until a skewer inserted into the centre comes out clean.

8. Remove from the oven and, while still piping hot, pierce the cake in several places with the skewer and pour over about 20ml of rum and 10ml of brandy to help preserve it. Set it on a wire rack to cool in the tin before turning out.

9. Once fully cooled, wrap in baking parchment or greaseproof paper and then an outer layer of foil and store in a cool, dry place for at least three weeks to allow the flavours to intermingle before cutting. Every week to 10 days, unwrap carefully and top up with another 30ml of alcohol before wrapping up again and storing.

10. Before serving, you can top with marzipan and/or royal icing. If using the marzipan, lightly dust a rolling pin and work surface with icing sugar and roll out the marzipan into a circle slightly larger than the cake. Whisk one of the egg whites and spread on the cake's surface before placing the marzipan on top.

11. For the royal icing, lightly whisk the remaining egg whites in a large, clean mixing bowl, sieving in the icing sugar little by little as you whisk. Keep whisking for about 10 minutes or until you have thick peaks, then fold in the glycerine and whisk a little further to integrate fully. Spread onto the cake with a spatula or palette knife.

Simplest Fruit Cake Ever

KITTY HARRINGTON, FRENCHPARK GUILD, ROSCOMMON

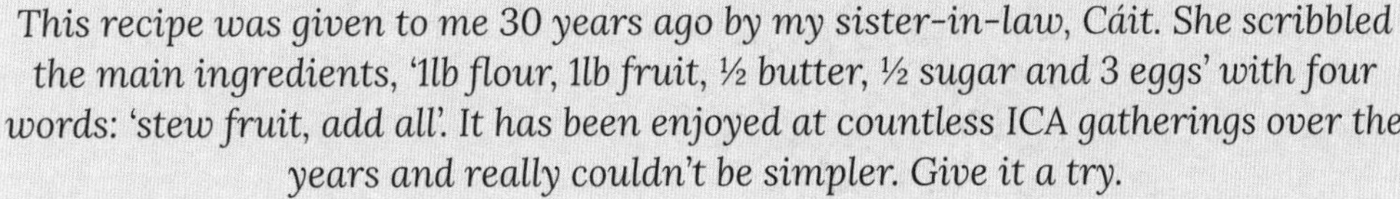

This recipe was given to me 30 years ago by my sister-in-law, Cáit. She scribbled the main ingredients, '1lb flour, 1lb fruit, ½ butter, ½ sugar and 3 eggs' with four words: 'stew fruit, add all'. It has been enjoyed at countless ICA gatherings over the years and really couldn't be simpler. Give it a try.

Makes one large or two small loaves

- 450g (1lb) mixed dried fruit
- 225g (8oz) butter
- 225g (8oz) caster sugar
- 450g (1lb) plain flour
- 1 heaped teaspoon baking powder
- ½ teaspoon mixed spice
- 3 eggs, lightly beaten
- 50g (2oz) chopped walnuts
- 50g (2oz) mixed peel (optional)

what you'll need

- 900g (2lb) loaf tin
  or
  2 x 450g (1lb) loaf tins
- baking parchment
- wire rack

1. Preheat oven to 170°C/325°F/Gas 3. Grease one or two loaf tins and line with baking parchment.

2. In a large, heavy-based saucepan, cover the fruit with cold water, bring to the boil and simmer gently for five minutes. Strain and return the fruit to the saucepan.

3. Return the saucepan to a very a low heat, add the butter and sugar and keep stirring until the butter has melted and the sugar is fully dissolved. Set aside to cool for at least five minutes.

4. Sieve the flour, baking powder and spice together into a large mixing bowl. Once the wet mixture is cool to touch, stir this into the flour mixture, mix well and then add the lightly beaten eggs. Tip in the walnuts and peel, if using, and mix through.

5. Transfer to the prepared tin/tins and bake in the preheated oven for 60 minutes or until a skewer inserted in the centre comes out clean.

6. Remove from the oven and leave in the tin to cool for a few minutes before transferring to a wire rack to cool fully. Wrap in greaseproof paper and store in an airtight container, where it will keep for a few days or up to a week.

Tea Brack

ANNE MCDONAGH, MULLINGAR GUILD, WESTMEATH

This simple tea brack is a favourite. The recipe requires you to pre-soak the fruit overnight, but other than that its preparation is very straightforward and produces great results, with a good rise and delicious flavours. Tea brack should be served sliced, slathered in good butter and washed down with a hot cup of tea.

Makes one 900g (2lb) loaf

- 350g (12oz) mixed dried fruit
- 275ml (½ pint) cold tea
- 125g (4½ oz) caster sugar
- 1 egg
- 225g (8oz) self-raising flour
- a pinch of mixed spice (and/or ground cinnamon)

what you'll need

- 900g (2lb) loaf tin
- palette knife or spatula
- wire rack

ICA Tip

For a variation on this recipe, you could replace 100g (3½oz) of the dried fruit with an equal weight of roughly chopped walnuts and/or goji berries, adding them in the next day with the beaten egg.

1. In a large mixing bowl, combine the dried fruit and cold tea. Cover and leave overnight to soak.
2. The next day, preheat oven to 170°C/325°F/Gas 3. Generously grease a 900g (2lb) loaf tin with oil.
3. Stir the sugar into the soaked fruit. Whisk the egg until light and frothy and add to the fruit mixture. Sieve the flour and spices into a separate bowl before folding them into the large mixing bowl a spoonful at a time. Mix well and pour into the greased loaf tin, smoothing over the top with a palette knife or spatula.
4. Bake in the preheated oven for about an hour or until risen and firm to the touch.
5. Remove from the oven and allow to cool in the tin for 10 minutes before turning out on to a wire rack to cool fully.
6. Wrap in greaseproof paper and store in an airtight container, where it will develop more depth of flavour. This will keep for up to a week and is delicious toasted, if serving later in the week.

HOW TO MINIMISE FOOD WASTE

1. Fruit cake lasts well, especially those dense cakes that are packed full of preserved fruit and alcohol. It's important to wrap them extremely well too, ideally in an inner layer of baking parchment or greaseproof paper and then an outer layer of tinfoil, and finally in an airtight container such as Tupperware or a cake tin. Never wrap the cake directly in tinfoil as the foil may react with the fruit.

2. Often bread is best eaten fresh on the day it is baked, but even when it begins to tire all is not lost. To refresh bread rolls, preheat the oven to its highest temperature, moisten the roll quickly under the cold tap and pop in the oven for three minutes.

3. Stale bread and leftover heels can be transformed into breadcrumbs by drying out in the oven before blitzing with some chopped herbs and storing in an airtight container or resealable bag in the freezer.

4. Leftover ends of cheese can be grated and frozen in an airtight container for up to three months: defrost in the fridge before kneading into a savoury bread dough. Homemade jams are a great way to use up an excess of seasonal fruits, and can transform a simple Swiss roll, fresh scones or homemade soda bread into something special. See *The ICA Cookbook* for recipes and ideas.

5. Leftover egg yolks are useful for making fresh mayonnaise and aioli. To make mayonnaise, beat two seasoned egg yolks with a tablespoon of Dijon mustard and slowly drizzle in 275ml (½ pint) of oil while still whisking; once the yolks and oil begin to emulsify, add vinegar or lemon juice to taste. Leftover egg yolks are best used fresh but can be covered with a little cold water and refrigerated for a couple of days.

6. Over-ripe bananas are ideal for baking into delicious banana bread (see page 29). You can easily freeze them too: just mash them first and freeze as ice cubes which you can later bag up, or simply peel them and freeze whole in freezer bags.

7. Always label things properly before freezing, and include the date as well as a description. Three months is a good rule of thumb for keeping most frozen items. Keep some masking tape and a permanent marker handy for homemade labels.

8. Remember when cooking for a crowd that people eat less at a buffet-style meal than they would in a sit-down meal, so don't overestimate quantities. If you have a lot of leftovers, provide some parchment and foil for wrapping to encourage guests to take some home with them.

Chapter 3
Savoury Breads

Good Earth Yeast Bread

MARION LYON, MAGHERA GUILD, CAVAN

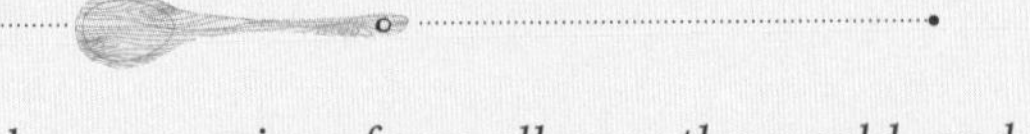

I love to bake and have collected many recipes from all over the world, and baking tips from various friends from far and wide. This sweet, treacle-based bread recipe is adapted from Evan Jones's wonderful cookbook, American Food: The Gastronomic Story. *I have replaced the active dry yeast with instant yeast.*

Makes two large loaves

- 180g (6oz) rolled oats
- 95g (3.5oz) cracked wheat
- 25g (1oz) wheat germ
- 725ml (1¼ pint) boiling water
- 225g (8oz) treacle
- 2 tablespoons melted butter
- 1½ tablespoons salt
- 1 teaspoon sugar
- 2 x 7g sachets instant dried yeast (fast action or rapid rise)
- 265ml (8½fl oz) milk
- 450g (1lb) stoneground wholewheat flour
- 450g (1lb) plain flour, sieved

to finish

- 50g (2oz) butter, for greasing
- 1 tablespoon vegetable oil, for oiling
- 1 egg white
- 1 tablespoon water

what you'll need

- 2 x 900g (2lb) loaf tins
- clean tea towel
- cling film

ICA *Tip*

Reduce the treacle if you prefer it less sweet.

1. In a large mixing bowl, soak the rolled oats, cracked wheat and whea germ in the boiling water. Add the treacle, melted butter, salt and su mix well and set aside to cool to body temperature (approx. 36°C).

2. Add the instant yeast and milk to the steeped oat mixture and mix w Add the wholewheat flour in two batches, incorporating the first be adding the next, then sieve in two-thirds of the plain flour and mix i a sticky dough.

3. Turn out onto a floured work surface. Allow to rest for a few minute then start kneading, adding more of the remaining plain flour as needed to achieve a firm, pliable consistency; it will be sticky, so do do much kneading at this time.

4. Generously grease a large mixing bowl with butter. Place the dough the bowl and turn it around to coat with butter; cover with a clean towel and allow to rise in a warm place, such as a hot press, until it doubled in size. (About two hours but judge by size rather than time

5. Punch down the risen dough (see page 191), turn out onto a floured surface and knead well for about 8–10 minutes, adding more flour a necessary. Halve the dough and form into two loaves. Grease both tins with butter and fill each with a loaf of dough. Cover with a clea tea towel or oiled cling film and leave somewhere warm to allow th dough to rise – it should almost double in size so that it swells over tops of the tins, about 30 minutes. Meanwhile, after about 15 minut preheat oven to 190°C/375°F/Gas 5.

6. When the dough is ready, brush with a wash of egg white mixed wi a tablespoon of water. Bake in the preheated oven for 15 minutes, t reduce the heat to 180°C/350°F/Gas 4 and continue baking for 30 minutes or until the base sounds hollow when knocked.

7. Remove the loaves from the pans and return them to the oven. Tur the heat and let the bread cool in the oven to obtain a nice crust.

Sourdough Bread

MIRIAM MURPHY, BLANCHARDSTOWN GUILD, DUBLIN

This recipe is an adaptation of a recipe from baker Patrick Ryan of Firehouse Bakery in Delgany, but adjusted to my own tastes. I like to make my starter with just flour and water, but you'll find lots of alternative techniques online with additions of yoghurt and milk or grated apple to kickstart the fermentation. You could cheat by sourcing the starter elsewhere (see tip for ideas) but if you are making your own, it is essential to use organic flour.

Makes two loaves

for the starter

- 700g organic strong white flour
- warm water

for the bread

- 500g organic strong white flour, plus extra for dusting
- 225ml warm water
- 1 teaspoon fine salt
- 1 tablespoon clear honey
- 300g sourdough starter

for greasing

- vegetable oil (something neutral in flavour)

what you'll need

- large (1 litre) sterilised jar with a screw top lid or plastic container with lid
- stand mixer with dough hook (optional)
- cling film
- proving basket or medium-sized bowl
- large baking tray
- small roasting tin
- wire rack

1. To make your starter, begin by whisking 100g flour with 125ml slightly warm water in a large mixing bowl until smooth.
2. Transfer the starter into a large (1 litre) clean jar with a screw-top lid or into a plastic container. Place somewhere warm (a hot press is good, or near a warm oven) for 24 hours, leaving the lid off for the first hour.
3. For the next six days, you will need to 'feed' the starter. Each day, discard half of the original starter, add an extra 100g flour and 125ml slightly warm water and stir well to combine. Try to do this at the same time every day.
4. After three or four days, bubbles should appear on the surface and the aroma should become yeasty and a little acidic – all good signs that the starter is working. By day seven, the starter should be quite bubbly and smell much sweeter. It is now ready to be used in baking.

***

5. To make the bread, sieve the flour into a large mixing bowl, add the warm water along with the salt, honey and 300g sourdough starter. Stir with a wooden spoon to bring it together into a dough. (Alternatively, you can do this in a stand mixer on a slow setting with a dough hook). Add a little extra water if the dough seems too dry, or extra flour if it is a bit sticky.

ICA Tip

If you don't want to go to through the week-long process of making your own starter, you could do as I sometimes do and use one that somebody else made, such as a friend or your local friendly baker (check realbreadireland.org for your locality).

6. If kneading by hand, tip onto a lightly floured surface and knead for 10 minutes until soft and elastic (it's a good idea to put a timer on). It should be able to stretch very thin without tearing. If using a mixer, turn up the speed a little and mix for five minutes.

7. Place the dough in a large well-oiled bowl and cover the bowl with oiled cling film. Leave in a warm place, such as a hot press or by a warm oven, to rise for three hours. You may not see much movement but don't let that put you off as sourdough takes much longer to rise than ordinary yeast breads.

8. Tip the dough out again onto a lightly floured work surface and knead briefly to knock out any air bubbles. Shape the dough into the required shape and dust very generously with flour. Place the dough 'seam' side down into a proving basket (alternatively, simply line a medium-sized bowl with a clean tea towel and flour it very generously).

9. Cover the bowl loosely with a sheet of oiled cling film and leave at room temperature until it has roughly doubled in size. This will take anything from four to eight hours, depending on variables such as the strength of your starter and the temperature of the room. The best indicators are your eyes, so don't worry too much about timings.

10. When ready to bake the bread, place a large baking tray in the oven and preheat to 230°C/450°F/Gas 8. Fill a small roasting tin with a little water and place this in the bottom of the oven to help create some steam, which will help the crust to form. Remove the baking tray from the oven, sprinkle with flour and then carefully tip the risen dough directly onto the tray.

11. Slash the top of the loaf about three times at an angle with a very sharp knife. Bake for 30–40 minutes until it is golden brown and the base sounds hollow when knocked. Transfer to a wire rack and allow to cool for 20 minutes before slicing.

Quick White Yeast Bread

NOELINE POWER, TRAMORE GUILD, WATERFORD

This white yeast bread uses a fast action dried yeast, which can be added directly into the flour without activation. It requires just one proving and isn't knocked back like some yeast-based breads. My children always loved it when I added a simple water-based sugar icing on top, but that's entirely optional!

Makes one large loaf or two small loaves

- 450g (1lb) strong white flour, plus extra for dusting
- 1 level teaspoon salt
- 1 level teaspoon sugar
- 25g (1oz) margarine
- 1 x 7g sachet instant dried yeast (fast action or rapid rise)
- 275ml (½ pint) tepid water

what you'll need

- 900g (2lb) loaf tin
  or
  2 x 450g (1lb) loaf tins
- stand mixer with a dough hook (optional)
- cling film
- wire rack

ICA Tip

Unlike dried active yeast, modern dried instant yeast can be added directly without needing to be activated in liquid first. However, some bakers believe that you get a better proof by rehydrating the dried yeast in the tepid water first before adding to the dried ingredients.

1. Generously grease a 900g (2lb) loaf tin or two 450g (1lb) loaf tins.

2. Sieve the flour and salt into a large mixing bowl, then stir in the sugar. Add the margarine and rub in with your fingers until it resembles breadcrumbs.

3. Stir in the yeast, mix well and then add three-quarters of the tepid water, which should be one part hot to two parts cold. Mix the whole lot into a pliable dough, adding extra water if needed, but taking care not to let it become too sticky.

4. Turn onto a floured board or work surface and knead (see page 69) for about 10 minutes or until smooth and elastic. Alternatively, you could knead it in a mixer with a dough hook for about five minutes.

5. Shape the dough, dividing it in two if baking in two tins, and then place it into the prepared loaf tin(s). Cover with oiled cling film and leave to prove for about two to four hours or until the dough has at least doubled in size.

6. Preheat oven to 190°C/375°F/Gas 5.

7. Bake in the loaf tin(s) in the preheated oven for about 30 minutes or until golden on top and the base sounds hollow when knocked.

8. Remove from the oven and allow to cool in the tin(s) for a few minutes before transferring to a wire rack to cool fully.

Wheatmeal Bread

JOAN MCLOUGHLIN, CAPPAMORE GUILD, LIMERICK

This recipe is a perfect project for a rainy day when you want to stock up the freezer with some healthy homemade bread. It's a little time-consuming to make but the finished bread rewards your efforts with a great rise. I like to use granola from The Happy Pear in Greystones, Co. Wicklow.

Makes two large loaves

- 25g (1oz) instant dried yeast (fast action or rapid rise)
- 850ml (1½ pint) water, approx.
- 900g (2lb) wholemeal flour
- 450g (1lb) plain flour
- 4 heaped tablespoons granola
- 25g (1oz) salt
- 50g (2oz) butter, cubed (or lard or vegetable shortening such as Cookeen)
- 25g (1oz) caster sugar

what you'll need

- 2 x 900g (2lb) loaf tins
- clean tea towel

ICA Tip

This bread toasts and freezes well, so it makes a good one to slice before freezing and then simply defrost and toast slices as needed.

1. Preheat oven to 220°C/425°F/Gas 7. Grease two 450g (1lb) loaf tins. Dissolve the yeast in about 150ml (¼ pint) of lukewarm water.

2. Measure the wholemeal flour into a large mixing bowl, sieve in the plain flour and mix in the granola and salt. Rub in the butter or lard with your fingers until you have a crumb-like texture, then stir in the sugar.

3. Make a well in the dry ingredients and add the dissolved yeast and the rest of the measured water; mix with a wooden spoon or your floured hands to give a fairly soft dough, adding more water if necessary.

4. Tip out onto a lightly floured surface and knead for 7–10 minutes until smooth and elastic. Flour the mixing bowl and return the dough to it. Cover with a clean tea towel and leave to rise in a warm place, such as a hot press or by a warm oven, for two hours or until it has doubled in size.

5. Turn onto a floured board or worktop, knead lightly and then shape into two loaves to fit the prepared tins. Divide the dough between the tins and set aside to prove again for 20–30 minutes or until the bread fills the tins.

6. Bake towards the top of the preheated oven for about 15 minutes, then reduce the temperature to 200°C/400°F/ Gas 6 and continue cooking for another hour or until the base sounds hollow when knocked. Remove from the oven and turn out onto a wire rack to cool before slicing.

Onion and Sage Focaccia

MARGARET REDMOND, PORTLAOISE GUILD, LAOIS

My family loves this bread, which is particularly delicious served warm. We love this combination of flavours but feel free to experiment takes your fancy, using different herbs or vegetables (cherry tomatoes, rosemary, garlic and olives all work well). I usually bake it in a larger cake tin but you can opt for a smaller one if you prefer a thicker focaccia.

Makes one small loaf

- 210ml (7½fl oz) lukewarm water
- 1 tablespoon olive oil
- 350g (12oz) strong white flour, plus extra for dusting
- ½ teaspoon salt
- 1 tablespoon caster sugar
- 1 teaspoon dried instant yeast (rapid rise or fast action)
- 1 tablespoon chopped fresh sage
- 1 tablespoon chopped red onion

for the topping

- 2 tablespoons olive oil
- 2 teaspoons coarse sea salt
- ½ red onion, finely sliced
- a few fresh sage leaves

what you'll need

- stand mixer with dough hook
- rolling pin
- clean tea towel
- round cake tin, between 20cm–28cm (8in–11in)
- cling film
- wire rack

1. Pour the lukewarm water and oil into your stand mixer. Sprinkle over the flour, trying to cover the water. Add the salt and sugar to opposite sides of the bowl. Make a small indent in the flour and add the yeast.

2. Knead with the dough hook for five minutes, or until the dough is smooth and elastic. Transfer to a clean oiled bowl, cover with a clean tea towel and set aside to rise for about an hour.

3. When the dough has doubled in size, place it on a lightly floured or oiled worktop. Knock back the dough (see page 69) and flatten it slightly. Sprinkle over the chopped sage and red onion and knead gently to incorporate. Shape the dough into a ball, flatten it, then roll it into a round about the size of your tin.

4. Lightly oil your round cake tin and place the dough inside. Cover with oiled cling film and leave to rise in a warm place, such as a hot press or near a warm oven, for 20 minutes.

5. Uncover the risen focaccia, and poke the dough with your fingertips to make about a dozen deep hollows over the surface. Cover and leave to rise for 10–15 minutes, or until the dough has doubled in bulk. Meanwhile preheat oven to 200°C/400°F/Gas 6.

6. Before baking, add the toppings: drizzle over the olive oil and sprinkle with the salt, onion and a few whole sage leaves. Bake in the preheated oven for 20–25 minutes or until golden. Transfer to a wire rack to cool slightly before serving warm.

Italian Stromboli Bread

EDWARD HAYDEN, ICA COOKERY TUTOR, GRAIGUENAMANAGH, KILKENNY

Edward Hayden is a chef and cookery tutor whose popular recipes have been shared with ICA members for years through his cookery demos and also with wider readers through this series of ICA cookbooks. This versatile bread recipe is delicious as described here, but can also be used in various ways (see tip overpage).

Makes one very large loaf

- 450g (1lb) strong flour, plus extra for dusting
- 12g (½oz) salt
- 25g (1oz) fresh yeast (or 1 x 7g sachet fast action yeast, such as McDougall's)
- 300ml (10fl oz) hand-hot water (35–37°C)
- 2 teaspoons olive oil

for the filling

- 1½ peppers (red and yellow/green), de-seeded and diced into bite-sized pieces
- 1 red onion, peeled and diced into bite-sized pieces
- 12 cherry tomatoes
- 1 tablespoon olive oil
- 3 bacon rashers
- 85g (3oz) mozzarella cheese, grated

1. Line a baking sheet with baking parchment. Sieve the flour and salt into a large mixing bowl, stirring to mix, then make a well in the centre.

2. In a small bowl, stir the yeast into the hand-hot water to dissolve. Pour in the oil and add this mixture to the flour. Mix to combine and then turn out onto a lightly floured surface. Knead for about 7–10 minutes in order to achieve elasticity, by which time the dough should have all come together into a smooth ball.

3. Transfer to a large oiled or floured bowl and cover with cling film or a clean tea towel until the dough has doubled in size, usually 50–60 minutes. After about 30 minutes, preheat oven to 190°C/375°F/Gas 5.

4. To prepare the filling, spread the diced peppers, red onions and whole cherry tomatoes on a baking tray, drizzle with a little oil and bake in the preheated oven for 15 minutes until softened. Meanwhile, lightly grill the bacon and dice into bite-sized pieces. Set the fillings aside while you prepare the dough.

5. Remove the cling film from the proving bowl and gently punch the risen dough to deflate it. Transfer to a lightly floured surface and knead for another 30 seconds or so.

6. With a lightly dusted rolling pin, roll the dough into a large rectangular shape and brush all the way around the edge with some egg wash to create a border. Scatter the

→

for the egg wash

- 1 egg, beaten with a little milk

what you'll need

- baking tray
- baking sheet
- baking parchment
- cling film or clean tea towel
- rolling pin
- pastry brush

ICA *Tip*

You can roll out this dough thinly to create pizza bases, or bake it in a 900g (2lb) loaf tin for a simple yeast-based bread.

central area with the roasted vegetables, diced bacon and grated cheese. Ensure that the filling is kept a little shy of the dough's edges.

7. Roll up the dough as you would a Swiss roll or roulade. Squash the dough a little to ensure that the filling is not too loose and seal the ends by tucking the borders in and under.

8. Transfer carefully to the lined baking sheet. Brush the top with a little egg wash, dust with additional flour and bake in the preheated oven for 40–45 minutes or until firm to the touch. Allow to cool slightly on the tray before slicing as required.

Cheese Bread

MARION LAWLESS, PORTLAOISE GUILD, LAOIS

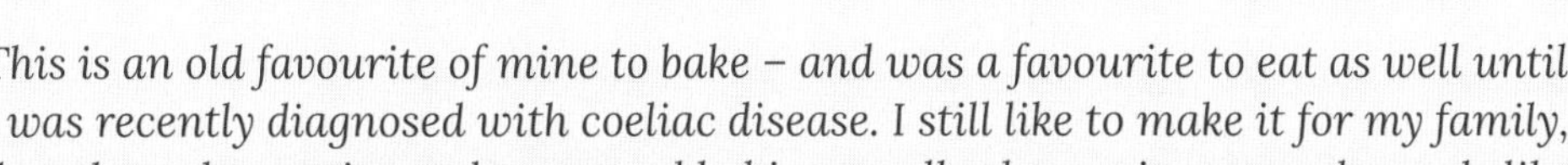

This is an old favourite of mine to bake – and was a favourite to eat as well until I was recently diagnosed with coeliac disease. I still like to make it for my family, though, and sometimes play around baking smaller loaves in unusual vessels like terracotta flower pots to produce several smaller, taller loaves.

Makes two large loaves
- 450g (1lb) strong flour
- 1 teaspoon salt
- 200ml (7fl oz) warm water
- 2 x 7g sachets instant dried yeast
- 1 egg, beaten
- 110g (4oz) mature Cheddar, grated

to finish
- 50g (2oz) butter, melted

what you'll need
- 900g (2lb) loaf tin
- clean tea towel
- pastry brush
- wire rack

1. Preheat oven to 180°C/350°F/Gas 4. Grease a 900g (2lb) loaf tin.

2. Sieve the flour and salt into a large mixing bowl. Make a well in the centre and set aside.

3. In a jug, combine the warm water and instant yeast, mix well and set aside to cool. Once the yeast and water have cooled, add the beaten egg and mix well.

4. Add the wet ingredients to the dry ingredients and mix to create a stiff dough, adding a little more flour if necessary. Turn out onto a lightly floured surface.

5. Knead for 5–10 minutes or until it becomes elastic, adding extra flour as needed to prevent the dough from sticking.

6. Place the dough in the greased loaf tin and cover with a clean tea towel. Set aside somewhere warm to prove for two hours, by which time it will have doubled in size. Turn the dough back out onto a floured surface, scatter with the grated cheese and gently incorporate the cheese by kneading it into the dough. Return the dough to the loaf tin to prove again for a further 15 minutes.

7. Bake the bread in the preheated oven for 45–55 minutes, or until the crust is crispy and golden brown and the base sounds hollow when knocked.

8. Remove from the oven and turn out from the tin onto a wire rack. Brush the butter on with a pastry brush, cover with a clean tea towel and leave to cool fully. Enjoy sliced, slathered with lots more butter.

Herb, Courgette and Tomato Bread

ANNE GABBETT, MUNGRET ST PAULS GUILD, LIMERICK

This tasty, savoury and gluten-free bread is delicious served on its own but goes particularly well with soup. You can use whatever herbs take your fancy, but basil, oregano, thyme, lemon thyme or tarragon would all work well.

Makes one large loaf or two small loaves

- 450g (1lb) gluten-free self-raising flour
- 2 tablespoons chopped fresh herbs, such as thyme and rosemary (or 2 teaspoons dried mixed herbs)
- ½ teaspoon salt
- 300ml (10fl oz) milk
- 2 tablespoons sunflower oil
- 1 egg, beaten
- 1 medium-sized courgette, unpeeled and grated
- 125g (4½oz) cherry tomatoes (about 8), sliced or quartered

what you'll need

- 900g (2lb) loaf tin
  or
  2 x 450g (1lb) loaf tins
- wire rack

1. Preheat oven to 200°C/400°F/Gas 6. Generously grease your loaf tin/tins with oil.
2. Sieve the flour into a large mixing bowl, add the herbs and salt and mix well with a metal spoon.
3. Add the milk, oil and beaten egg together with the grated courgette and sliced tomatoes and mix well to incorporate fully into a wet mixture, adding a little more milk if necessary.
4. Spoon the mixture into prepared loaf tin(s) and bake on the middle shelf of the preheated oven for about 40 minutes or until a fine skewer inserted into the centre comes out clean.
5. Allow to cool on a wire rack before removing from the tin(s).

ICA Tip

When cooking for gluten-intolerant people, and most especially coeliacs, take great care to avoid any contact with gluten-containing ingredients or cooking utensils that could have any traces of gluten.

Porridge and Yoghurt Bread

MARIE O'TOOLE, PORTMARNOCK GUILD, DUBLIN

You can convert this wheat-free bread to fully gluten-free by sourcing gluten-free porridge oats, which are widely available and not contaminated by other gluten-containing grains during their processing. Use the empty yoghurt tub to measure out the oats, for convenience.

Makes one large loaf

- 1 x 500g (1lb 2oz) tub natural yoghurt, empty tub reserved
- 1 egg, beaten
- 2–3 tablespoons milk
- 2–3 tablespoons olive oil
- 375g (13oz) porridge oats (*gluten-free if desired), or 2 yoghurt tubs' worth
- 1 teaspoon bicarbonate of soda
- ¼ teaspoon salt
- 100g (3½oz) dried fruit or mixed seeds

what you'll need

- 900g (2lb) loaf tin
- wire rack

1. Preheat oven to 200°C/400°F/Gas 6. Grease a 900g (2lb) loaf tin.
2. Mix all the wet ingredients (the first four) together in one large mixing bowl, using just two tablespoons each of the milk and olive oil. Mix all the dry ingredients in a second bowl, including the dried fruit or seeds, if using.
3. Fold the dry ingredients into the wet ingredients, mixing until well combined into a wet dough, and adding an extra tablespoon of milk and/or olive oil if needed.
4. Transfer the mixture to your greased loaf tin and bake in the preheated oven for about 45–50 minutes. Remove from the oven and loosen with a palette knife to remove from the tin (using a dry tea towel to handle the hot tin) and turn the bread upside-down in the tin. Return to the oven for a further 10 minutes to crisp up the bottom.
5. Remove to a wire rack to cool completely before slicing.

ICA *Tip*

Adding seeds like sunflower, pumpkin or sesame seeds provides extra crunch and helps to lighten the texture of the bread, while a teaspoon or two of milled linseed (flax) will improve the moistness of this recipe. Dried fruit like raisins, goji berries, cranberries or chopped dried apricots or prunes provide extra sweetness and flavour.

Savoury Tea Bread with Bacon and Apple

ETHNA DRUDY, FRENCHPARK GUILD, ROSCOMMON

This savoury bread makes a great addition to a light evening meal, served cool with lots of cold salted butter and washed down with a hot cup of tea.

Makes one small loaf

- 110g (4oz) lean bacon rashers, finely chopped
- 2 apples, peeled, cored and chopped
- 1 small onion, peeled and very finely chopped
- 225g (8oz) self-raising flour
- a pinch of salt
- a few turns of black pepper from a pepper mill
- 25g (1oz) butter or margarine
- 1 egg
- 80ml (3fl oz) milk, approx.

what you'll need

- 450g (1lb) loaf tin
- wire rack

1. Preheat oven to 190°C/375°F/Gas 5. Grease a 450g (1lb) loaf tin and line the base with parchment.

2. Heat a little oil in a heavy-based frying pan and fry the chopped rashers over a medium heat together with the apples and onion for 5–10 minutes or until the onions have softened and the apples have broken down. Remove from the heat and set aside to cool.

3. Sieve the flour and salt into a large mixing bowl, grind in the black pepper and then rub in the butter with your fingers until you have a crumb-like texture. Add the cooled rasher, apple and onion mix to incorporate and make a well in the centre.

4. In a small bowl, beat the egg together with the milk and mix this into the flour mixture. You may need to add another tablespoon or two of milk to bind it together into a stiff, sticky dough.

5. Spoon the dough into the prepared loaf tin and bake in the preheated oven for 40 minutes or until the base sounds hollow when knocked.

6. Remove from the oven and leave in tin to cool for a few minutes before turning out onto a wire rack to cool fully. Serve sliced, spread with butter.

Savoury White Loaf with Bacon and Cheese

MARGARET REDMOND, PORTLAOISE GUILD, LAOIS

Though it takes a little time, this yeast-baked bread is very achievable. I use a stand mixer as I have arthritis, but feel free to knead it by hand. I like to dissolve the yeast in milk and sugar in the traditional way that is used to activate dried active yeast, even though I use instant yeast which doesn't need to be activated.

Makes one large loaf

- 450g (1lb) strong white flour
- ½ teaspoon salt
- 250ml (8fl oz) milk
- 1 teaspoon dried instant yeast (rapid rise or fast action)
- 1 teaspoon sugar
- 3 bacon rashers, chopped (or 40g/1½oz bacon lardons)
- 12g (½oz) butter, or ½ tablespoon vegetable oil, for frying
- 1 egg
- 2 heaped tablespoons (40g/1½oz) grated mozzarella
- 2 heaped tablespoons (40g/1½oz) grated mature or sharp Cheddar
- a dash of Worcestershire sauce

what you'll need

- stand mixer with dough hook (optional)
- 900g (2lb) loaf tin
- baking parchment
- 2 x clean tea towels
- wire rack

1. Sieve the flour and salt into a stand mixer fitted with a dough hook, if using, or into a large mixing bowl.

2. Gently warm the milk in a saucepan, taking care not to bring it to the boil. Remove from the heat, add the yeast and sugar, stir well to dissolve and set aside for a few minutes to cool. Meanwhile, fry the chopped bacon or lardons in a little butter or oil, drain on kitchen paper and set aside.

3. Beat the egg into the milk-yeast mixture. Add to the flour and mix on a medium speed for five minutes with the dough hook, or bring together in the bowl with your hands and then transfer to a lightly floured surface and knead by hand for five minutes.

4. Transfer the dough into a clean, oiled bowl, cover with a clean tea towel and leave somewhere warm to rise for an hour. After about 45 minutes, preheat oven to 200°C/400°F/Gas 6 and grease a 900g (2lb) loaf tin and line with baking parchment.

5. After this first proving, knock back the dough (see page 69). In a small bowl, mix the cooked bacon with the grated cheeses and Worcestershire sauce, and knead these into the dough until well incorporated into a nicely elastic dough.

6. Increase the oven heat to its highest temperature. Roll and shape the dough to fit the prepared loaf tin and bake in the preheated oven until the dough has risen to the top of the tin, about 30 minutes. Reduce the temperature to 200°C/400°F/Gas 6 and bake for another 20 minutes or until the base sounds hollow when knocked.Remove from the oven and turn out onto a wire rack to cool fully. For a softer crust, wrap in a clean tea towel while cooling.

HOW TO MASTER BREAD-MAKING

1. Freshly baked Irish soda bread is quick and easy to make and no kneading is required. Its leavening (the factor that makes it rise) is achieved through the activation of alkaline bicarbonate of soda (bread soda) by an acidic ingredient such as buttermilk, sour milk or yoghurt.

2. In recent years, Irish bakers have embraced bread-making traditions from around the world, which add new challenges – working with yeast or natural sourdough starters, for instance, requires more skill and time commitment from the baker.

3. It's crucial to source and use the right ingredients. If your recipe calls for strong flour, you can't replace it with regular flour; the high gluten content of strong flour will be integral to achieving the rise that gives bread its lightness. Strong flour is widely available and can be picked up in most supermarkets.

4. Yeast is available in different forms. The most common type is instant dried yeast, sometimes called 'fast action', 'rapid rise', 'easy blend', 'easy bake' or 'quick' yeast. Instant yeast comes in small 7g sachets and often includes additives such as wheat flour, wheat starch, salt and bread improvers like ascorbic acid (a component of vitamin C). You can add this modern dried yeast straight to the flour, although some bakers prefer to add it to a liquid such as lukewarm water first.

5. 'Dried active yeast' is dried, granulated yeast that does not contain improvers or additives. It needs to be 'activated' before use by putting it in lukewarm water along with some sugar to feed the yeast. After five or 10 minutes, the mixture will bubble, which is a sign that the activation has been successful.

6. Fresh yeast is alive and ready to be blended in lukewarm water with no need for activation. It should be refrigerated and ideally used within a few days. You can source fresh yeast from specialist shops such as Dublin's Irish Yeast Company, health food stores, Polish shops or perhaps ask nicely at your local baker or craft pizzeria.

7. Kneading, proving (the time allowed for the dough to rise) and punching down are all crucial steps in the formation of gluten. They help to produce an elastic dough that can stretch as the air pockets expand during baking, giving bread its all-important rise and crumb structure.

8. Set a timer for the required time and knead on a lightly floured surface, using the heel of your hand to push the dough away from you before folding it back towards you. The final dough should be smooth rather than sticky.

9. Follow the recipe instructions regarding proving and punching down (the act of releasing some trapped air). Slashing the top of the dough with a sharp knife before baking encourages an even rise. Fully cooked bread should feel light and sound hollow when knocked on its base.

Chapter 4
Scones, Bread Rolls & Crackers

Simple Scones

MARY TIMMINS, BALLYCONNELL GUILD, CARLOW

I have made scones from many recipes, but this is the recipe I have been asked to share with so many who have tasted them. As the saying goes, 'the proof of the pudding is in the eating'.

Makes 20 medium-sized scones

- 500g (1lb 2oz) self-raising flour, plus extra for dusting
- 2 teaspoons baking powder
- 250g (9oz) cold butter, cubed
- 25g (1oz) caster sugar
- 1 egg
- 200ml (7fl oz) milk

to glaze

- a little extra milk or beaten egg

to serve

- good Irish butter
- raspberry jam
- whipped cream (optional, but highly recommended)

what you'll need

- baking tray
- baking parchment
- rolling pin
- scone cutter
- pastry brush
- wire rack

1. Preheat oven to 200°C/400°F/Gas 6. Line a baking tray with parchment.

2. Sieve the flour and baking powder together into a large mixing bowl, then rub in the butter with your fingers until you have a crumb-like texture. Stir in the sugar and make a well in the centre.

3. Beat the egg and milk in a small bowl with a fork, pour this into the well in the dry ingredients and use a knife to work it into a dough; it should be soft, but not sticky.

4. Dust a rolling pin and work surface lightly with flour and roll the dough out to a thickness of about 2cm (¾in). Cut out with a scone cutter and transfer to the lined baking tray.

5. Brush each scone with a little milk or beaten egg and bake in the preheated oven for about 15–18 minutes, or until risen and golden.

6. Remove from the oven and leave in the tin on a wire rack to rest for five minutes while you boil the kettle for tea. Eat with butter and raspberry jam – and maybe a dollop of whipped cream!

7. These will keep for several days in an airtight container.

ICA Tip

If your dough becomes too sticky, you can add a little more flour to rebalance it.

Currant Scones

MÁIRE UÍ MHURCHU, CUMANN NA CLOCHÁN BRÉANAIN, CIARRAÍ

This is a very old family recipe handed down through generations and is ideal for a novice cook to try. The scones are delicious served freshly baked for an afternoon tea with lashings of butter. The recipe makes a large quantity, but you could freeze some of these before or after baking (page 87) or halve the ingredients (and mix the spare half an egg with a little milk to glaze the scones before baking).

Makes 24 scones

- 675g (1½lb) plain flour
- 1 teaspoon baking powder
- 1 teaspoon bicarbonate of soda
- ½ teaspoon mixed spice
- ½ teaspoon cinnamon
- ½ teaspoon ginger
- ½ teaspoon nutmeg
- 225g (8oz) cold butter, cubed
- 375g (13oz) currants or raisins
- 110g (4oz) caster sugar
- 3 eggs
- 125ml (4fl oz) buttermilk
- 1 teaspoon treacle

what you'll need

- baking tray
- baking parchment
- rolling pin
- scone cutter
- pastry brush
- wire rack

1. Preheat oven to 180°C/350°F/Gas 4. Line a baking tray with parchment.
2. Sieve the flour, baking powder, soda and spices together into a large mixing bowl, then rub in the butter until you have a crumb-like texture. Fold in the fruit and sugar and make a well in the centre.
3. Beat the eggs in a small bowl with the buttermilk and treacle, then work it into the dry ingredients with a knife to bind it together into a sticky dough.
4. Dust a rolling pin and work surface lightly with flour and roll the dough out to a thickness of about 2cm (¾in). Cut out with a scone cutter and transfer to the parchment-lined baking tray.
5. Bake in the preheated oven for 20–25 minutes or until risen and golden.
6. Remove from the oven onto a wire rack and allow to rest for at least five minutes before serving. These will keep well for several days in an airtight container.

ICA Tip

You can also bake this as a currant loaf – a cross between a light cake and a dense bread: simply transfer the dough into two 450g (1lb) loaf tins and bake at 170°C/325°F/Gas 3 for 50–60 minutes. It will keep well for up to a week.

Potato and Herb Scones

ANNE GABBETT, MUNGRET ST PAULS GUILD, LIMERICK

This simple recipe is a great way to use up leftover potatoes. Delicious served hot, maybe to accompany a lunchtime or teatime salad, these wholesome scones are equally delicious eaten cold, making them ideal for school lunch boxes and picnics. They're also endlessly versatile, so once you master the basic recipe you can start to have fun with variations (see tip).

Makes 8 medium-sized triangle scones

- 75g (6oz) mashed potatoes (roughly 1 medium potato)
- 225g (8oz) plain flour
- 2 teaspoons baking powder
- ¼ teaspoon salt
- 50g (2oz) cold butter, cubed
- 1 tablespoon chopped fresh herbs, or 1 teaspoon dried herbs
- 2–3 tablespoons fresh milk or cream

what you'll need

- baking sheet
- wire rack

ICA Tip

Have fun with the herbs that you use: fresh parsley or basil work well, while dill, tarragon, oregano or thyme are also good to use either fresh or dried. For variation, you can also add finely chopped vegetables such as courgette or red onion.

1. If making the mash from scratch, simply peel the potato, dice into chunks and steam or boil at a rolling simmer until tender, then mash and season with salt and freshly ground black pepper.

2. Preheat oven to 190°C/375°F/Gas 5. Lightly grease a baking sheet.

3. Sieve the flour, baking powder and salt into a large mixing bowl and rub in the butter until you have a crumb-like texture.

4. Make a well in the centre and use a butter knife to mix in the mashed potatoes and herbs with a little milk or cream. Once it starts to come together gather it up in your hands to create a manageable dough.

5. Turn onto a lightly floured board or work surface, shape into a round of about 1cm (½ in) thick and cut into eight triangles.

6. Bake on the greased baking sheet in the preheated oven for about 20–25 minutes or until lightly browned and risen, checking during cooking and lowering the heat if the scones seem to be browning too quickly.

7. Remove from the oven onto a wire rack and allow to rest for at least five minutes before serving.

Wholemeal Scones

JOAN DUNNE, TRADAREE GUILD, CLARE

There are days when you want a scone that is wholesome, hearty and a good team player. This one would be a great accompaniment to a homemade soup, or perhaps sliced in half, toasted and served with strong farmhouse Cheddar and your favourite chutney.

Makes 8–10 medium-sized scones

- 285g (10oz) wholemeal flour
- 110g (4oz) plain flour
- 85g (3oz) wheat bran
- 1 teaspoon bicarbonate of soda
- a pinch of salt
- 50g (2oz) margarine (or cold butter, cubed)
- 1 egg
- 1 small tub natural yoghurt (approx. 110g/4oz)
- a little milk (about 1 tablespoon)

what you'll need

- baking tray
- baking parchment
- rolling pin
- scone cutter
- pastry brush

1. Preheat oven to 190°C/375°F/Gas 5. Line a baking tray with parchment.

2. Mix all the dry ingredients (the first five) together in a large mixing bowl, then rub in the margarine until you have a crumb-like texture. Make a well in the centre.

3. Beat the egg, yoghurt and milk in a small bowl with a fork, pour this into the dry ingredients and use a knife to work the mixture into a soft dough.

4. Dust a rolling pin and work surface lightly with flour and roll the dough out to the desired thickness – about 2cm (¾in) is usually good. Cut out with a scone cutter and transfer to the lined baking tray.

5. Bake on the middle shelf of the preheated oven for 25 minutes or until risen and golden.

ICA Tip

The added bran in this recipe is an easy way of increasing your intake of fibre.

Fresh Yeast Bread Rolls

MARIE O'TOOLE, PORTMARNOCK GUILD, DUBLIN

These simple white bread rolls are a great introduction to baking with fresh yeast. The recipe works well without the ascorbic acid (a component of vitamin C) so feel free to leave it out. However, if you want to experiment with this bread improver, the addition of which supports the development of crumb structure, you'll find it in specialist food stores.

Makes 20 white bread rolls

- 25g (1oz) fresh yeast
- 25mg ascorbic acid (optional, available from specialist food stores)
- 400ml (14fl oz) warm water
- 675g (1½lb) plain flour, plus extra for dusting
- 2 level teaspoons salt
- 1 level teaspoon caster sugar
- 25g (1oz) margarine

what you'll need

- large polythene bag (or large bowl and cling film)
- stand mixer with dough hook (optional)
- 2–3 x flat baking trays or sheets, lightly greased
- wire rack
- palette knife

ICA Tip

Fresh yeast can be hard to get your hands on; besides specialist shops such as Dublin's Irish Yeast Company, you can seek it out from health-food stores or Polish shops or perhaps befriend your local baker or craft pizzeria.

1. Preheat oven to 200°C/400°F/Gas 6. Grease a large polythene bag and two to three flat baking trays with oil. Alternatively, you could replace the bag with a large greased bowl and cling film. Add the yeast (and ascorbic acid, if using) to the warm water, and set aside.

2. Sieve the flour and salt into a large mixing bowl, mix in the sugar and rub in the margarine with your fingers until you have a crumb-like texture. Add the yeast mixture and mix together with a palette knife to create a dough.

3. Turn out onto a lightly floured board and knead by hand for 10 minutes, lightly stretching the dough away from you with the heel of your hand and folding it back towards you (see page 69). Alternatively, you can knead the dough in a stand mixer with a dough hook for about five minutes or until smooth and elastic.

4. Place the dough in the greased polythene bag (or in a large well-greased bowl and cover with greased cling film). Set aside to rest for five minutes.

5. Remove the dough from the bag (or bowl, if using, and reserve the cling film). Divide into 20 equal pieces, rolling each into a ball with the palm of your hand. Place them onto the lightly greased baking trays, spaced at least 2.5 cm (1in) apart. Cover with the greased bag or cling film and leave to prove for another 20–25 minutes.

6. Bake in the preheated oven for 15–20 minutes or until the base of the rolls sound hollow when knocked. Remove from the oven and transfer to a wire rack to cool.

Oatcakes

RENA MCCLEAN, TAUGHBOYNE GUILD, DONEGAL

These oatcakes are lovely with cheese or with butter and jam. I often make these for my husband, who is diabetic, and when I do I simply omit the sugar.

Makes 18 oatcakes

- 110g (4oz) plain flour
- ½ teaspoon bicarbonate of soda
- 50g (2oz) butter, cubed
- 225g (8oz) pinhead oatmeal
- 25g (1oz) caster sugar
- ½ teaspoon fine sea salt

what you'll need

- baking sheet or tray
- baking parchment
- rolling pin
- large cookie cutter
- wire rack

ICA Tip

You could swap some of the pinhead oats for sesame seeds, maybe about 25g (1oz).

1. Preheat oven to 180°C/350°F/Gas 4. Lightly grease the baking sheet or tray, or line with parchment.
2. Sieve the flour and soda into a large mixing bowl. Rub in the butter with your fingers, then add the rest of the ingredients and mix well before binding together with just enough boiling water to make a stiff dough (about four tablespoons).
3. Roll out thinly onto a floured surface and cut into circles or triangles. Transfer to the prepared baking sheet or tray.
4. Bake in the preheated oven for about 15–18 minutes or until cooked through or golden and crispy.
5. Remove from the oven and leave on the tray to cool for a few minutes before transferring to a wire rack to cool fully.
6. Store in an airtight container where they will keep well for about a week.

Rye Crackers

SUE WARDELL, TINAHELY GUILD, WICKLOW

Rye is an ancient grain that is naturally low in gluten (but not gluten-free) and produces dense breads with a distinctive flavour, which these tasty, crisp crackers share. They are excellent with cheese and can be baked plain or with added flavourings. They keep very well so you could double the recipe and make half of the dough with flavourings and half without or with a different flavouring for contrast.

Makes about 30 crackers

- 150g (5½ oz) rye flour
- 75g (2½oz) plain flour, sieved
- ½ teaspoon salt
- 1 tablespoon oil
- 125ml (4fl oz) water (approx.)

to flavour (optional)

- 1 tablespoon cumin seeds, sesame seeds, or finely chopped rosemary

what you'll need

- baking sheet
- pasta machine (or rolling pin and elbow grease)
- wire rack
- chef ring/cookie cutter (optional)

ICA Tip

As well as being lower in gluten than wheat flour, rye flour is higher in soluble fibres, making it good for your gut health too.

1. Preheat oven and baking sheet to 220°C/425°F/Gas 7.
2. Mix the dry ingredients in a large mixing bowl along with any optional flavouring you wish to add, and make a well in the centre.
3. Stir in the oil and enough water to bring the mixture together into a manageable dough – it shouldn't be too sticky. Cover the bowl and refrigerate for 20–30 minutes.
4. If you have a pasta machine handy, use it to roll out small quantities of the dough. Start on the thickest setting, then the middle setting and finish on the second thinnest setting. Alternatively, you can use a rolling pin and a bit of elbow grease, but you want to get these as thin as possible – no more than ½ cm (¼in) thick.
5. Cut into your desired shape, either with a knife for triangles, rectangles or squares, or with a round cookie cutter or chef ring. If using a round cutter, you can then re-roll the remaining dough. An 8cm (3in) chef ring is perfect for creating crackers for a cheese board and will give you about 30 crackers in total (20 in the first roll and 10 from the re-roll).
6. Lightly flour the preheated baking sheet and lay the crackers out on the sheet (don't worry if they are close to each other as they won't expand widthways). Bake in the preheated oven for 6–8 minutes or until dry and crisp and slightly risen.
7. Remove from the oven and leave on the baking sheet to cool slightly before transferring to a wire rack to cool fully. Store in an airtight container where they will keep well for a couple of weeks at least.

HOW TO BAKE SCONES

1. The best scones are made by hand, so don't be tempted to mix them in a machine – they become dense and claggy, which is not the effect you're looking for!

2. Irish butter is the best in the world, so feel free to swap it in for margarine for extra flavour.

3. Working with cold rather than room-temperature butter will help to give a nice rise to your final scones.

4. Add a handful of sultanas, currants or mixed fruit with candied peel to a simple scone recipe to make fruit scones, mixing them into the flour before you add the liquid. You may want to decrease the sugar quantity in the recipe to rebalance the sweetness.

5. Always hold back on some of the liquid to allow you to judge when you've added enough. Ingredients like flour behave differently depending on lots of variables – including our fickle Irish weather – and it's much easier to add more liquid than to try and rebalance with extra flour. You're aiming for a dough that holds together without crumbling, but that isn't overly sticky to handle.

6. Work with cold, lightly floured hands and avoid over-mixing your dough as this will cause the scones to become hard and dense.

7. Dipping your scone cutter into flour before using will stop the dough sticking to the cutter (especially if your dough has erred on the sticky side) and will help to give clean edges. If you don't have a scone cutter, you can use the rim of a glass instead – or shape the dough into a square or rectangle and cut into triangles, but take care not to over-handle the dough, as above.

8. If you have a little beaten egg left over, use it to glaze the scones before baking. You can mix it with some milk to make it go further.

9. Preheating the baking tray and baking in a fully preheated oven will help give your scones a nice crust and good rise.

HOW TO FREEZE SCONES

1. One of the nicest things you can serve to a visitor is a freshly baked scone, but the reality is we don't always have the time to whip something up on the day we'd like to serve it. This is where your freezer comes in especially handy: you can freeze a batch of baked scones, and then defrost in the microwave – and we've suggested a couple of other options below.

2. If you have a reasonably sized freezer, consider making a large batch of scones, as on page 75, or simply by doubling up smaller recipes, and freezing half of them.

3. If your freezer has enough free space, you could prepare and cut out the dough into individual scones, lay these out on a parchment-lined baking tray and freeze them for an hour or two. Then transfer them to a Ziploc bag for more efficient storage in your freezer, where they'll be good for up to three months. Don't forget to label the scones with the date so you know when to use them by.

4. If your freezer lacks the space for the above approach, bake the scones as per the recipe and cool fully before stacking carefully into an airtight container and freezing. They won't have the same shelf life, however, so you'll want to use them within a month.

5. For the first method, simply bake the scones from frozen as per the original recipe's oven temperature and timings, but allowing an extra few minutes for the scones to defrost. You can have the smell of freshly baking scones wafting through the house within 20 minutes of your guest's arrival, and you can have them on the table within about 40 minutes – just in time for that second pot of tea!

6. For the second method, simply pop the pre-baked scones straight into the microwave for about five minutes or until piping hot – ideal for an impromptu visitor.

7. Alternatively, gently defrost pre-baked scones at room temperature for about an hour before baking in a preheated oven at 170°C/325°F/Gas 3 for about 5–7 minutes, or until a sharp knife or skewer inserted into the centre comes out hot.

Chapter 5
Biscuits & Bites

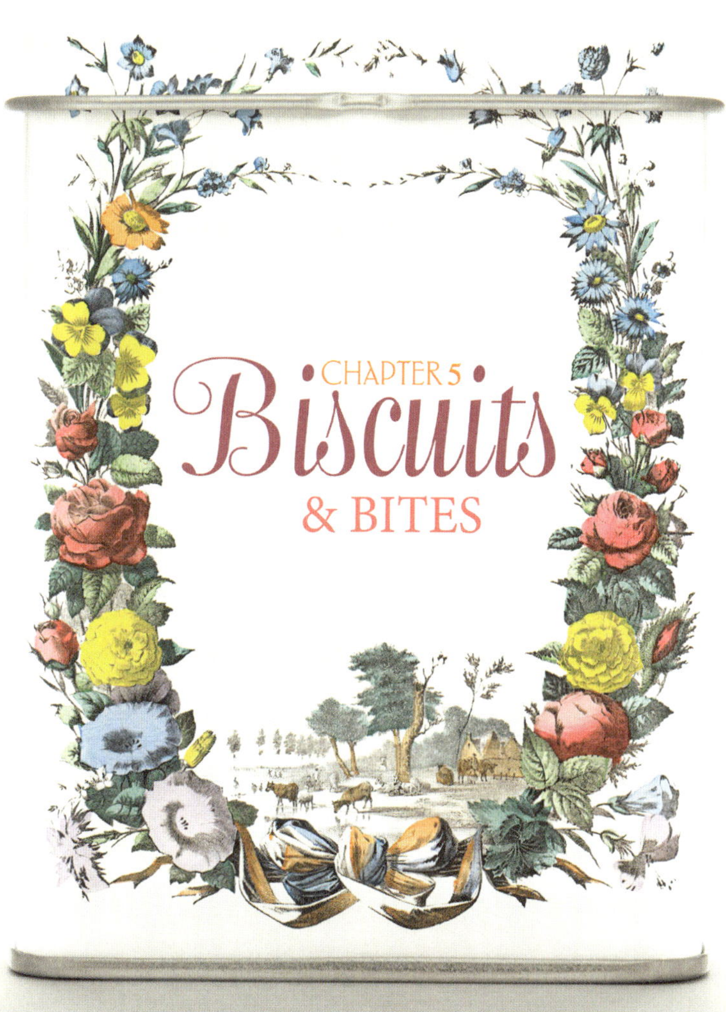

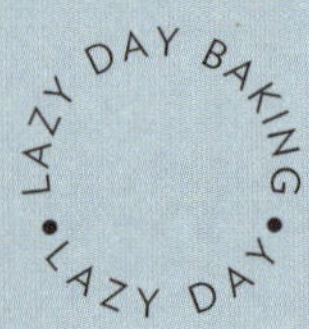

Apple Biscuits

MICHELLE EARLY, AUGHAVAS GUILD, LEITRIM

This clever and unusual traybake is one to make on a lazy Sunday when you have a bit of time on your hands. The fresh apple filling adds an extra layer of flavour as well as texture. It can be cut into biscuits large or small, depending on how you'd like to serve them, or can even be served as a warm dessert with custard or cream.

Makes 12 squares or 24 fingers

- 4 cooking apples
- juice of ½ lemon
- 225g (8oz) softened butter
- 225g (8oz) caster sugar
- 4 eggs, beaten
- 2 teaspoons vanilla extract
- 350g (12oz) plain flour
- 2 teaspoons baking powder
- 1 tablespoon milk (optional)

to finish

- 1–2 tablespoons Demerara sugar

what you'll need

- baking tray
- parchment paper
- stand mixer (optional)
- wire rack

ICA Tip

Scoring the batter before baking will make the biscuits easier to cut once cooled.

1. Preheat oven to 150°C/300°F/Gas 2. Line a flat baking sheet with parchment paper.
2. Peel, core and thinly slice the apples. Place in a bowl and squeeze over the lemon juice to prevent the apples oxidising and browning.
3. Beat the butter and sugar together in a large mixing bowl or stand mixer, then add the beaten eggs and vanilla and beat in to incorporate. Mix in the flour and baking powder with a wooden spoon, adding a tablespoon of milk if the batter is too thick.
4. Spread half of the mixture into the parchment-lined baking tray, and arrange the sliced apples over the batter before topping with the remaining mixture.
5. Sprinkle Demerara sugar over the top and bake in the preheated oven for 50–60 minutes or until browned all over.
6. Remove from the oven and allow to cool on a wire rack before cutting into biscuit or square shapes. Store in an airtight container where they will keep well for a few days. Alternatively, serve them warm with custard or cream.

Date Biscuits

HILDA ROCHE, ASHFORD GUILD, WICKLOW

My mum was a great baker and this was one of my favourites – I was always hoping to find one in my lunch box! As well as being naturally sweet, dates are high in fibre and rich in vitamins and minerals. These crunchy biscuits are a clever way of getting these healthy fruits into anyone's diet, young or old.

Makes 16

- 110g (4oz) margarine
- 110g (4oz) caster sugar
- 1 egg
- 170g (6oz) self-raising flour
- 300g (10½oz) pitted dates, chopped

to finish

- 50g (2oz) cornflakes, lightly crushed on a plate

what you'll need

- flat baking tray or sheet
- baking parchment
- wire rack

1. Preheat oven to 180°C/350°F/Gas 4. Line a baking tray with parchment.

2. Cream the margarine and sugar in a large mixing bowl. Beat in the egg, stir in the flour and chopped dates, and form into individual balls – you'll get about 16 at around the size of a golf ball.

3. Roll each ball of dough in a little crushed cornflakes and bake on the prepared baking tray in the preheated oven for about 15–20 minutes or until the biscuits themselves (not just the cornflakes) have turned golden and crunchy on the outside.

4. Remove from the oven and allow to cool on a wire rack.

Chewy Chocolate Chip Cookies

ELEANOR CALNAN, LEAP GUILD, CORK

Who doesn't love chocolate chip cookies, especially when they are nicely chewy like these tasty versions? This recipe makes a versatile base that you can change up with the addition of extra ingredients like caramelised ginger, a pinch of cinnamon powder, flaked almonds or chopped nuts.

Makes about 24 large cookies

- 250g plain flour
- ½ teaspoon baking soda
- a pinch of salt
- 170g (6oz) unsalted butter
- 225g (8oz) brown sugar
- 110g (4oz) caster sugar
- 3 teaspoons vanilla extract
- 2 eggs
- 340g (12oz) chocolate chips

what you'll need

- 2 x baking sheets
- parchment paper
- wire rack

ICA Tip

If you're in a hurry, you can simply spoon a tablespoon each of dough directly onto the lined or greased baking sheet without leaving the dough to stand and then rolling them into balls.

1. Grease the baking sheets or line with parchment paper.
2. Sieve the flour and baking soda into a large mixing bowl, stir in the salt and set aside.
3. Melt the butter, combine it with the brown and caster sugar in another large mixing bowl and mix together thoroughly. Add the vanilla and eggs and beat until light and creamy. Fold in the sieved dry ingredients with a wooden spoon, then stir in the chocolate chips.
4. Leave the dough to stand for 30 minutes, and preheat oven to 170°C/325°F/Gas 3. Roll the dough with your hands into small balls of about a tablespoon each. Place them well spaced onto the prepared baking sheets. Bake in the preheated oven for 15–17 minutes, or until the edges are lightly brown.
5. Allow to cool on the baking sheets for a few minutes before transferring the cookies to a wire rack to cool completely. Store in an airtight container where they will keep well for a week or so.

Ginger Biscuits

ANN SMITH, RAPHOE GUILD, DONEGAL

These fast and easy egg-free biscuits taste lovely and are so much nicer to serve with cup of tea or coffee than a shop-bought biscuit. I got the recipe from a Scottish aunt many years ago. You need very little equipment to make them and they cook very quickly. Using a vegetable shortening like Cookeen makes these vegan-friendly, or you could use butter if you prefer.

Makes 24 small biscuits

- 170g (6oz) plain flour
- ½ teaspoon bicarbonate of soda
- ½ teaspoon ground ginger (or 1 teaspoon for a stronger ginger flavour)
- 50g (2oz) caster sugar
- 1 tablespoon golden syrup
- 50g (2oz) vegan margarine
- 50g (2oz) vegetable shortening like Cookeen (or butter, if you prefer)

what you'll need

- baking tray
- parchment paper
- wire rack

ICA Tip

If you like your ginger biscuits to have a good crunch, bake them for the full 10 minutes until dark golden all over. Alternatively, for a softer texture, cover your just-baked biscuits with a tea towel while cooling.

1. Preheat oven to 180°C/350°F/Gas 4. Line a baking tray with parchment.
2. Sieve the flour, soda and ginger into a large mixing bowl, then stir in the sugar.
3. Melt the syrup with the margarine and Cookeen (or butter), and add to the dry ingredients. Mix together to combine well.
4. Scoop up a teaspoonful of this mixture and roll it into a small ball. Place on the prepared baking tray and flatten the top with a fork. Repeat with the remaining mixture, ensuring the biscuits are well spaced out as they will expand when baked.
5. Cook in the preheated oven for 7–10 minutes, keeping a close eye on them for the last few minutes as they burn easily. Remove from the oven and leave on the tray to cool for a few minutes before transferring to a wire rack to cool fully.
6. Store in an airtight container where they will keep well for a week or so.

Marmalade Shortcakes

FRANCES MURRAY, BELTRA GUILD, SLIGO

Having a good shortcake recipe up your sleeve is useful in itself, but this recipe brings things to another level by layering two biscuits into a sandwich with the addition of a tangy marmalade in the centre.

Makes about 8 layered biscuits

- 225g (8oz) plain flour
- 85g (3oz) caster sugar
- a pinch of salt
- 110g (4oz) butter (cubed) or margarine
- 1 tablespoon milk
- 120g (4½oz) marmalade, approx.

what you'll need

- baking sheet
- baking parchment
- rolling pin
- cookie cutter, ideally one large (approx. 5–6cm/2–2½in) and one small (1.5cm/¾in), or improvise as in the method)
- spatula or spoon for spreading marmalade
- wire rack

ICA Tip

You're aiming for 16 biscuits in total; if you do run short, you could re-roll the leftover dough from the perforated biscuits but try to handle the dough with a light touch to avoid it toughening.

1. Preheat oven to 140°C/275°F/Gas 1. Lightly grease a baking sheet, or line with baking parchment.
2. In a large mixing bowl, combine the flour, sugar and salt and mix well.
3. Rub in the margarine or butter until it is evenly distributed, then add the milk and knead to a smooth dough.
4. On a lightly floured surface, roll the dough out to a thickness of about ½cm (¼in) and cut into approximately 16 round biscuits using a large cookie cutter if you have it, or alternatively use the rim of a glass.
5. Mix the marmalade with a very small amount of hot water to loosen it, and then spread about a teaspoon of marmalade each onto half of the biscuits.
6. In the centre of the remaining biscuits, cut three small round holes with a small cookie cutter (you'll need something about the size of a euro coin; alternatively, use the smallest cookie cutter you have to cut one hole rather than three). Place the perforated biscuits on top of the marmalade-covered biscuits.
7. Bake in the preheated oven on the prepared baking sheet for about 40 minutes or until the shortcakes are a pale golden colour. Remove from the oven and leave on the baking sheet to cool for a few minutes before transferring to wire rack to cool fully. Store in an airtight container where they will keep for a few days.

Oat and Honey Crunch Biscuits

EILEEN BAMBRICK, DRUMBOYLAN GUILD, ROSCOMMON

Crunchy and slightly chewy, these biscuits are delicious served with your morning coffee. Just one or two will certainly do, though, as they are quite rich. You can simply double up the ingredients if you'd like to make a larger batch.

Makes 12 biscuits

- 110g (4oz) softened butter, plus extra for greasing
- 110g (4oz) caster sugar
- 1 teaspoon clear honey
- 1½ tablespoons hot water
- 110g (4oz) rolled oats
- 110g (4oz) plain flour
- ½ teaspoon baking powder
- ½ teaspoon bicarbonate of soda

what you'll need

- 2 x large baking sheets
- wire rack

ICA Tip

Lightly dampen your hands before flattening the balls of dough onto the baking sheets – this will prevent the dough sticking to your skin.

1. Preheat oven to 190°C/375°F/Gas 5. Grease two large baking sheets with a little butter.

2. In a large mixing bowl, cream the butter and sugar together until soft and creamy. Add the honey and hot water and stir to combine. Add the oats and sieve in the flour, baking powder and soda. Mix everything together well.

3. Use two spoons to shape the dough into 12 balls (about the size of a golf ball) and flatten these onto the greased baking sheets, placing just six on each tray and spreading well apart – they will expand while cooking.

4. Bake in the preheated oven for 10–15 minutes or until golden all over.

5. Remove from the oven and leave to cool fully on the baking sheets for 10 minutes before using a spatula to transfer to a wire rack to cool fully.

6. Store in an airtight tin where they will keep well for about a week.

Grantham Gingerbread Biscuits

CARMEL DAWSON, BALLYCONNELL GUILD, CAVAN

The Grantham gingerbread biscuit is England's oldest biscuit recipe. Unlike the egg-free ginger biscuit on page 95, these are baked low and slow for a lovely crumbly biscuit.

Makes 12–14 biscuits
- 110g (4oz) margarine
- 110g (4oz) caster sugar
- 1 tablespoon beaten egg
- 110g (4oz) self-raising flour
- 2 teaspoons ground ginger

what you'll need
- baking tray
- baking parchment
- electric whisk or stand mixer
- wire rack

ICA Tip

If you prefer a darker biscuit, you could bake these for longer, up to about an hour.

1. Preheat oven to 150°C/300°F/Gas 2. Lightly grease a baking tray or line with parchment.
2. Cream together the margarine and sugar until smooth. Add the beaten egg and mix well to combine thoroughly.
3. Sieve the flour and ginger into the creamed mixture and beat to a stiff dough.
4. Scoop up a heaped teaspoon of the mixture and roll into a ball in the middle of your palm, then flatten it out and place onto the greased or lined baking tray. Continue until you've used up all the mixture.
5. Bake on the middle shelf of the preheated oven for 45 minutes.
6. Remove from the oven and leave in the tin to cool for a few minutes before transferring to a wire rack to cool fully.
7. Store in an airtight container where they will keep well for a week or so.

Apple Creams

SARAH MCDERMOTT, BALLINODE GUILD, SLIGO

These miniature tarts are lovely as a mid-morning treat or as part of a buffet spread for a gathering. You can prepare the tartlets and stewed apple in advance and easily assemble them with the whipped cream at the last minute.

Makes 12–16

- 110g (4oz) margarine
- 40g (1½oz) caster sugar
- 25ml (½ tablespoons) milk
- 170g (6oz) plain flour

for the stewed apples

- 2 medium apples
- 50g (2oz) caster sugar
- 1 tablespoon water
- a pinch of ground cinnamon, ginger or nutmeg (optional)

to finish

- 250ml (8fl oz) cream, freshly whipped

what you'll need

- 12-cup bun tin
- palette knife
- rolling pin
- large fluted cookie cutter
- piping bag (optional)

ICA Tip

This pastry can also be used to make iced biscuits. Simply bake the rounds of pastry on a greased or lined baking sheet and then use the icing recipe from page 104, or change to orange icing, using the rind and juice of an orange instead of a lemon.

1. Preheat oven to 180°C/350°F/Gas 4. Lightly grease a 12-cup bun tin.

2. Cream the margarine and sugar together in a large mixing bowl. Beat in the milk, then add the flour and blend in using a palette knife before bringing it together with your hands to form a pastry. Take care not to overwork it.

3. On a lightly floured surface, roll the pastry out fairly thinly, about ½cm (¼in). Cut with a fluted cookie or scone cutter and press into the tin so that they form little tartlets. This pastry will not rise and does not need to be pricked. Bake in the preheated oven for 15–20 minutes or until golden brown.

4. Meanwhile, for the stewed apples, peel, core and roughly chop the apples and combine them in a saucepan with the sugar, water and spices, if using. Cover and cook gently for seven or eight minutes or until nicely stewed (cooking apples will cook down to a smoother purée than eating apples, which will keep their form). Taste and adjust with a little more sugar or honey if too tart, or a little lemon juice if you prefer it a little sharper.

5. Remove the tartlets from the oven and allow to cool before filling each with stewed apple and decorating with whipped fresh cream; a piping bag is useful for making these look extra pretty but you could also work with a pair of spoons and make little quenelles of whipped cream (see page 191) or simply opt for a rustic look.

Easy Chocolate Fudge

EVELINE MCCANDLESS, CARNDONAGH GUILD, DONEGAL

This dangerously addictive but very straightforward fudge requires no sugar-work skill; instead its success hinges on the quality of the ingredients used, and in particular the chocolate, so don't skimp by compromising with cooking chocolate. Once you master this basic recipe, you could experiment with additions such as chopped nuts, desiccated coconut, sultanas, orange zest, goji berries or whatever else you fancy trying.

Makes 36 bite-sized squares

- 500g (1lb 2oz) good-quality dark chocolate, ideally at least 70% cocoa content
- 400g (14oz) can sweetened condensed milk
- 75g (2½oz) butter
- ½ teaspoon vanilla extract

what you'll need

- 20cm (8in) square cake tin
- spatula
- cling film

ICA Tip

The higher the cocoa content of the dark chocolate you use, the richer the fudge will be. Don't be tempted to use milk chocolate as the resulting mixture remains too sticky.

1. Lightly grease a 20cm (8in) square cake tin.

2. Break the chocolate into small pieces and place in a saucepan with the condensed milk and butter. Heat gently over a low heat until the chocolate and butter have melted and the mixture is smooth. Take care not to let it boil.

3. Remove from the heat. Add the vanilla extract and beat the mixture for a few minutes until it thickens.

4. Pour into the prepared tin and level the top with a spatula. Cover with cling film and refrigerate to set for at least two hours or ideally overnight.

5. Carefully tip the fudge out onto a board and cut into bite-sized squares of about 3.5cm x 3.5cm (1½in x 1½in).

6. Store in an airtight container where it will keep for a week or two, or for a few weeks if refrigerated.

Iced Lemon Squares

JANICE MCCANDLESS, CARNDONAGH GUILD, DONEGAL

This quick and clever no-bake recipe is a great example of how a little personal TLC can upgrade ordinary shop-bought biscuits and a few store-cupboard items into something quite special. The results are very sweet, so a bite-sized square works nicely. You could swap the lemon for lime, which would pair very well with the white chocolate as well as the coconut flavours of the biscuit base.

Makes 32 bite-sized squares

- 350g (12oz) Nice biscuits
- 225g (8oz) margarine
- 225g (8oz) white cooking chocolate
- 2 tablespoons golden syrup
- 110g (4oz) desiccated coconut

for the icing

- 285g (10oz) icing sugar
- 1 lemon, juice and grated rind

to garnish

- a little extra desiccated coconut, for sprinkling

what you'll need

- large Swiss roll tin, about 23cm x 33cm (9in x 13in)
- food processor (or clean tea towel & rolling pin)

1. Lightly grease a large Swiss roll tin.
2. Finely crush the biscuits in a food processor. Alternatively, place the biscuits between parchment or a clean tea towel and crush with a rolling pin.
3. Melt the margarine, white chocolate and syrup together in a medium-sized saucepan. Add the crushed biscuits and coconut and mix well to combine.
4. Press this biscuit mixture into the greased Swiss roll tin and set aside or refrigerate for 30 minutes to cool.
5. To make the icing, mix the icing sugar in a small bowl with the grated lemon rind. Add the lemon juice a little at a time until you have an icing that is of a fairly soft consistency; about 50ml of juice should do.
6. Cover the biscuit base with the icing and sprinkle with a little extra coconut. Allow to set fully before cutting into squares; 30 minutes in the fridge is perfect.

ICA Tip

When binding white chocolate with margarine like this, it is important to use good-quality chocolate as cheaper cooking chocolate can have a very high fat content, and may separate slightly. The addition of a little warmed milk can help to bring the two together.

Schokocrossies

CARMEL GARRETT, KNOCKNACARRA GUILD, GALWAY

My daughter lives in Germany and while I was staying with her there I first tried these Schokocrossies, or German rice crispie buns. I like to use milk chocolate but, for a richer flavour, you could mix half milk and half dark chocolate.

Makes 12

- 200g (7oz) good-quality chocolate
- 50g (2oz) flaked almonds
- 50g (2oz) cornflakes

what you'll need

- small bun cases
- heatproof bowl

ICA Tip

You can substitute pecans or peanuts for almonds: roughly chop them and toast on a dry pan over a low heat for about five minutes, tossing regularly. For a more grown-up variation, sprinkle with a little sea salt, or add a dash of Cointreau and garnish with finely grated orange rind.

1. Melt the chocolate either in a bowl in the microwave or in a bain marie (a heatproof bowl placed over a pot of simmering water).

2. Toast the flaked almonds to a golden brown. This can be done under a hot grill, in a preheated oven or on a dry hot pan, but take care not to burn them.

3. Mix the browned almonds with the cornflakes in a mixing bowl, pour the melted chocolate over and mix thoroughly.

4. Spoon the mixture into small bun cases and set aside to cool: either for an hour at room temperature, 30 minutes in the fridge or for 15 minutes in the freezer.

Marshmallow and Toffee Tartlets

RENA MCCLEAN, TAUGHBOYNE GUILD, DONEGAL

Although these tartlets are a bit fiddly I like to make them for special occasions. I make them for my brother at Christmas as he loves them, and I get a lot of teasing from my own family asking if he is coming when they see me making them!

Makes 12

for the pastry

- 175g (6oz) plain flour
- 110g (4oz) cold butter (or hard margarine), cubed
- 55g (2oz) caster sugar

for the filling

- ¼ jar raspberry jam
- 6 medium-sized marshmallows, halved horizontally
- 55g (2oz) butter (or hard margarine)
- 55g (2oz) caster sugar
- ½ tablespoon golden syrup
- 85g (3oz) sweetened condensed milk

to finish

- 100g (3½oz) milk chocolate
- 4 squares of white chocolate (optional)
- heatproof bowl

what you'll need

- 12-cup bun tin
- baking parchment
- rolling pin
- large scone or cookie cutters
- baking beans

1. Cut out 24 parchment discs and use half of them to fill the base of each cup of the bun tin.

2. To make the pastry, rub the flour, butter or margarine and sugar together in a mixing bowl until they resemble breadcrumbs. Add about a tablespoon of cold water and shape into a soft, smooth ball. Wrap the pastry in cling film and refrigerate for 20–30 minutes. Preheat oven to 170°C/325°F/Gas 3.

3. Dust a rolling pin and work surface lightly with flour and roll the pastry out to a thickness of about .5cm (¼in). Cut out rounds with a cutter and transfer into the bun tin, pressing into each hollow. You may need to re-roll each a little to fit it.

4. Cover the base of each tartlet with a parchment disc, pop a few baking beans into each to weigh it down and bake blind in the preheated oven for 15–20 minutes or until lightly browned and dry. Remove from the oven and set aside to cool.

5. Dollop half a teaspoon of jam into the base of each tartlet case, and top with half a marshmallow.

6. To make the toffee, melt the butter or margarine and sugar in a high-sided, heavy-based saucepan over a low heat. Add the syrup and condensed milk and slowly bring to the boil, stirring continuously. Cook, stirring, for 5–10 minutes or until the toffee leaves the side of the pan, then remove from the heat.

7. Spoon a little toffee into each tartlet, covering the jam and marshmallow. Allow to cool while you melt the milk chocolate; this can be done either in a bowl in the microwave or in a bain marie (a heatproof bowl placed over a pot of simmering water). Cover each tartlet with the melted chocolate. If using the white chocolate, melt as above and drizzle a little over each tartlet.

HOW TO IMPROVE YOUR BAKING

1. Baking is as much a science as it is an art, and while it offers plenty of opportunity for creative expression, it is important to master the basic principles of a recipe before you can experiment successfully. Follow the recipe precisely, pay particular attention to measurements and use a digital weighing scales where possible.

2. Remember, however, that oven temperatures vary and ingredients such as flour behave differently in different environments. Pay close attention where measurements or timings are given in degrees, such as adding only enough liquid to bring dry ingredients together into a dough, or baking for 50–60 minutes or until a skewer inserted into the centre comes out clean. In these cases, it is important to use the sensory information available to you and to file this information away for future reference.

3. Pay attention to the specific ingredients called for. While yeast-based breads require strong flour with a high gluten content, cakes typically require plain or self-raising flour. Don't be tempted to swap one for the other; however, if you don't have any self-raising flour to hand, you can mix up some by adding a teaspoon of baking powder to every 200g (7oz) plain flour. Commercial baking powder can be substituted with equal parts of bicarbonate of soda and cream of tartar (powdered tartaric acid).

4. When working with pastry, it's important to keep things cool – including your hands, your work space and surface (which is why bakers love marble counters) and your ingredients such as cold butter. Pastry should be handled lightly, kneaded as little as possible (to discourage the formation of gluten) and rested in the fridge before rolling. Pastry freezes well, if appropriately wrapped in cling film. Allow to defrost slowly at room temperature before using.

5. Once you master certain techniques such as blind baking pastry (see page 190) you can use these for various other recipes. Keep a small jar of dry beans for weighing down pastry during baking. These should be placed on top of a disc of baking parchment during the baking and are re-usable.

6. Remember that when baking cakes, scones and simple soda breads, it is important not to overwork the dough as you want to avoid the formation of gluten. This is unlike the approach to yeast- or starter-based bread-making, where we knead the dough to encourage gluten formation (see How to master bread-making, page 69). Likewise, pay attention to instructions such as folding, which is a gentle process of mixing dry ingredients into a wet mixture that has typically been beaten to incorporate plenty of air.

Chapter 6
Muffins & Buns

Bacon and Peanut Butter Muffins

MARION LYON, MAGHERA GUILD, CAVAN

Indulgence isn't just for those with a sweet tooth. These savoury muffins balance sweet and salty flavours and make a great choice for a mid-morning snack or lunch box addition along with some cheese and fruit.

Makes 12 muffins

- 300g (10½oz) plain flour, sieved
- 2 tablespoons (30g/1oz) caster sugar
- 1 tablespoon baking powder
- 1 teaspoon salt
- 2 tablespoons (2½oz) bacon fat or butter
- 1 egg
- 275ml (½ pint) milk
- 3 uncooked bacon rashers, finely chopped
- 2 heaped tablespoons (2½oz) peanut butter

what you'll need

- 12-cup muffin tin
- paper muffin cases (optional)
- wire rack

1. Preheat oven to 200°C/400°F/Gas 6. Lightly grease a 12-cup muffin tin or line with muffin cases.

2. Sieve the flour, sugar, baking powder and salt together in a mixing bowl.

3. Gently melt the bacon fat or butter. Meanwhile beat the egg in another large mixing bowl and whisk in the milk. Add the melted fat and chopped, uncooked bacon, and mix well. Stir in the flour mixture, but do not beat; the mixture should be just moistened.

4. Spoon out a little batter into each well of your muffin tin (or muffin case if using), then drop about a third of a teaspoon per muffin of peanut butter into each before topping up with batter to fill each well three-quarters full.

5. Bake in the preheated oven for 20–25 minutes or until risen and golden all over.

6. Remove from the oven and allow to cool in tin for a few minutes before transferring to wire rack to cool fully. These will keep for a day or two in an airtight container, or for a few months frozen if well-wrapped.

ICA Tip

For a sweet variation, reduce the salt to half a teaspoon, and replace the peanut butter and bacon with a cup of blueberries; you may not need quite as much milk to bind it so add half to start and then as much as you need after that.

Fruit and Nut Muffins

MICHELLE EARLY, AUGHAVAS GUILD, LEITRIM

These would make a nice treat to take on a hike and enjoy with a flask of hot tea or coffee – the inclusion of the dried fruit and nuts will provide some extra energy for the return leg.

Makes 12

- 300g (10oz) self-raising flour
- 1 teaspoon ground mixed spice
- 125g (4½oz) butter, softened
- 110g (4oz) caster sugar
- 2 eggs, lightly beaten
- 180ml (6fl oz) full-fat milk
- 200g (7oz) chopped dried fruit mix
- 70g (2½oz) chopped mixed nuts

what you'll need

- 12-cup muffin tin
- paper muffin cases (optional)
- palette knife
- wire rack

ICA Tip

The addition of chocolate chips would work very well, if you feel like making them extra indulgent. Simply swap out some of the dried fruits.

1. Preheat oven to 190°C/375°F/Gas 5. Lightly grease a 12-cup muffin tin or line with muffin cases.
2. Sieve the flour with the ground mixed spice into a large mixing bowl. In a separate bowl, cream together the butter and sugar, then rub this into the flour mixture with your fingers until you have a crumb-like texture.
3. Add the beaten egg and milk to bind everything together and finally fold in the fruit and nuts. Take care not to overmix.
4. Spoon the mixture into the prepared muffin tin. Bake for 20–25 minutes or until risen and golden, and a cocktail stick inserted into the centre comes out clean.
5. Remove the muffin tin from the oven and allow to cool a little before removing the muffins from the tin (if you haven't used cases, you can loosen them with a palette knife first). Allow to cool fully on a wire rack.
6. These will keep for a few days in an airtight container, or for a few months frozen if well wrapped.

Understanding Egg Codes
Production method as coded on egg

Gluten-Free Muffins

CARMEL DAWSON, BALLYCONNELL GUILD, CAVAN

When I was diagnosed with coeliac disease 36 years ago, gluten-free foods were very plain and drab. Thankfully nowadays there is a wide variety of delicious baked products available, but it can be nice to bake your own too. These simple muffins taste great by themselves but also make a handy base for various flavourings (see tip).

Makes 12

- 250g (9oz) gluten-free flour
- 2½ teaspoons gluten-free baking powder
- a pinch of salt
- 110g (4oz) butter, softened
- 110g (4oz) soft light brown sugar
- 2 medium eggs, beaten
- 150ml (¼ pint) milk
- sunflower oil, for greasing

what you'll need

- 12-cup muffin tin
- paper muffin cases (optional)
- wire rack

1. Preheat oven to 200°C/400°F/Gas 6. Generously grease a muffin tin with oil or line with paper cases.
2. Sieve the flour, baking powder and salt into a large mixing bowl. Add the butter and rub it in with your fingers until the mixture resembles breadcrumbs. Stir in the sugar and form a well in the centre.
3. Mix the beaten eggs with the milk in a small bowl, then add to the large mixing bowl and mix to form a smooth batter.
4. Pour the batter into the prepared cups of the tin and bake in the preheated oven for 12–18 minutes until risen and golden and the centre springs back when lightly pressed.
5. Remove the muffin tin from the oven and allow to cool a little before loosening the muffins from the tin. Transfer to a wire rack to cool a little further. Serve warm or cold.

ICA Tip

For a delicious variation on this basic recipe, add two tablespoons of raisins and half a teaspoon of ground cinnamon to the mixture before baking. Alternatively, you could add a handful or two of chocolate chip drops to the dough.

Mocha Muffins

MIRIAM MURPHY, BLANCHARDSTOWN GUILD, DUBLIN

These muffins are based on an all-in-one cake, which was one of the first I made as a child. The recipe was given to Mum by her sister, Ina Duigan, who was an avid member of Tullamore ICA from the 1960s until her untimely death in the 1980s. I always think of them both when I bake it.

Makes 12

- 170g (6oz) butter (or margarine), softened
- 170g (6oz) caster sugar
- 170g (6oz) self-raising flour
- 3 large eggs, beaten
- 1 tablespoon coffee essence* (Camp or Irel)
- 50g (2oz) chocolate chips, roughly chopped

for the coffee icing

- 110g (4oz) icing sugar
- 40g (1½oz) margarine or butter, melted
- 2 teaspoons milk
- 1 teaspoon coffee essence

to finish

- 25g (1oz) walnuts or pecans, roughly chopped or left whole

what you'll need

- 12-cup muffin tin
- muffin cases (optional but recommended)
- handheld or stand mixer
- palette knife
- wire rack

1. Preheat oven to 180°C/350°F/Gas 4. Lightly grease a 12-cup muffin tin or, preferably, line with muffin cases.

2. Combine the softened butter, sugar, flour, eggs and coffee essence in a bowl and beat with a mixer until well blended. (*If you cannot source coffee essence, you can use very strong instant coffee mixed with some boiling water – just make sure not to add too much liquid.) Fold in the chocolate chips.

3. Divide between the cups of the muffin tin and bake in the preheated oven for about 18–22 minutes or until risen and golden, and a cocktail stick inserted into the centre comes out clean.

4. Remove the muffin tin from the oven and allow to cool a little before removing the muffins from the tin (if you haven't used cases, you can loosen them with a palette knife first). Allow to cool fully on a wire rack before icing.

5. To make the icing, beat the icing sugar together with the butter or margarine, milk and coffee essence until blended smoothly. Use a palette knife to ice each muffin and top with a sprinkling of chopped pecans or walnuts.

ICA Tip

The same quantities can be used to make a sandwich cake baked in two 20cm (8in) sandwich tins, but you'll want to triple the quantity of the icing ingredients.

Linda's Breakfast Muffins

ELIZABETH MURPHY, BALLYROAN GUILD, LAOIS

Besides being speedy and straightforward to make, which is a plus in itself, the addition of fruit, nuts and coconut means that these delicious muffins are packed with natural goodness as well as natural flavour. As the name suggests, they are great at breakfast time with a hot cup of tea.

Makes 12 muffins

- 225g (8oz) self-raising flour
- 140g (5oz) caster sugar
- 1 teaspoon baking powder
- 50g (2oz) desiccated coconut
- 50g (2oz) chopped walnuts
- 50g (2oz) sultanas
- 1 carrot, peeled and grated
- 1 apple, peeled and grated
- 2 eggs
- 135ml (¼ pint) sunflower oil
- 1 teaspoon vanilla extract

what you'll need

- 12-cup muffin tin
- paper muffin cases (optional)
- wire rack

1. Preheat oven to 180°C/350°F/Gas 4. Lightly grease a 12-cup muffin tin or line with muffin cases.

2. Sieve the flour, sugar and baking powder into a large mixing bowl, add the coconut, walnuts and sultanas and mix well to combine.

3. Stir in the grated carrot and apple and mix well. Beat the eggs in a small bowl together with the sunflower oil and vanilla extract, fold in to the flour mixture and mix well to combine.

4. Divide the mixture equally between the cups in the prepared muffin tin and bake in the preheated oven for 25 minutes or until risen and golden, and a cocktail stick inserted into the centre comes out clean.

5. Remove from the oven and allow to cool in the tin for a few minutes before transferring to wire rack to cool fully. Will keep for a few days in an airtight container, or for a few months frozen if well-wrapped.

ICA Tip

This basic recipe can be altered to your tastes and needs – adding a pinch of ground nutmeg or cinnamon, perhaps; swapping the carrot and apple for courgette or pear; or swapping the walnuts for another nut like hazelnut, or indeed leaving out nuts for those with allergies.

Queen Cakes

FRANCES MURRAY, BELTRA GUILD, SLIGO

Before the world went mad for cupcakes, we used to have queen cakes or fairy cakes in our lives. These simple traditional treats would be a fun recipe to bake with young children.

Makes 12

- 85g (3oz) butter
- 110g (4oz) caster sugar
- 2 large eggs, beaten
- 170g (6oz) self-raising flour
- ½ teaspoon baking powder (optional)
- 85g (3oz) currants, well rinsed and patted dry
- a pinch of salt

what you'll need

- 12-cup bun tin
- paper cupcake cases (optional)
- wire rack

ICA Tip

If the butter and sugar start to curdle while beating in the egg, mix in a little of the flour, currants and salt.

1. Preheat oven to 200°C/400°F/Gas 6. Generously grease a 12-cup bun tin or line with cupcake cases.

2. Beat the butter and sugar to a cream. Add the beaten eggs little by little, beating in each addition thoroughly before adding any more. The final mixture should be stiff.

3. When all the egg is incorporated, sieve in the flour together with the baking powder, if using, and gently fold it in. Add the currants and salt and stir gently to incorporate fully.

4. Divide the mixture between the cups of the bun tin and bake in the preheated oven for 16–20 minutes or until golden.

5. Remove from the oven and allow to cool in the tin for a few minutes before transferring to a wire rack to cool fully.

Hot Breakfast Buns

KAY DEVINE, BONNICONLON GUILD, MAYO

Delicious and easy to make, these buns are served hot sprinkled with caster sugar and cinnamon. The recipe was given to me by my late Aunt Frances when I visited her in New Jersey in 2000. They are delicious anytime but especially in the morning with a hot cup of coffee.

Makes 12

- 3 tablespoons (85g/3oz) butter, melted
- 2 tablespoons margarine
- 150g (5½oz) caster sugar
- 1 egg
- 225g (8oz) plain flour
- 1½ teaspoons baking powder
- ½ teaspoon salt
- ¼ teaspoon ground nutmeg
- 125ml (4fl oz) milk

to finish

- 1 tablespoon caster sugar
- 1 teaspoon ground cinnamon
- 50g (2oz) butter, melted

what you'll need

- 12-bun muffin tin
- palette knife
- wire rack
- pastry brush

1. Preheat oven to 180°C/350°F/Gas 4. Use one tablespoon of the melted butter to grease a 12-bun muffin tin.

2. In a large mixing bowl, beat the remaining butter, margarine, sugar and egg until the mixture is smooth and creamy.

3. Sieve together the flour, baking powder, salt and nutmeg into a separate bowl and mix well. Beat this flour mixture, together with the milk, into the egg, sugar and fat mixture.

4. Spoon the batter into the greased muffin tin, filling each hollow two-thirds full. Bake in the oven for about 25 minutes or until the buns are risen and golden brown.

5. Remove from the oven and allow to cool slightly before removing the buns from the tin with a palette knife and turning out onto a wire rack. Mix the sugar and cinnamon in a small bowl. While the buns are still hot, brush with the melted butter and sprinkle with cinnamon sugar. Serve hot.

Orange Buns

PATRICIA GILLIGAN, SHEELIN GUILD, LOUTH

This recipe was given to my mother by her own mother years ago and was very popular in our house at harvest time. We always used orange marmalade, but you could experiment with different flavours of marmalade or jam if you prefer, or even use the same principle with a little leftover mincemeat around Christmas time.

Makes 12

- 225g (8oz) plain flour
- a pinch of salt
- 50g (2oz) softened butter
- 40g (1½oz) caster sugar
- 3 level teaspoons baking powder
- 1 egg
- 75ml (2½fl oz) milk
- 160g (5½oz) orange marmalade

to finish

- a little extra milk or beaten egg
- 1–2 tablespoons granulated sugar

what you'll need

- flat baking tray
- rolling pin
- 7½cm (3in) scone cutter
- pastry brush

1. Preheat oven to 200°C/400°F/Gas 6. Lightly grease a flat baking tray.
2. Sieve the flour and salt into a large mixing bowl and rub in the butter. Stir in the sugar and baking powder. Beat the egg and milk together, add to the mixing bowl and mix to a soft dough.
3. On a lightly floured surface, roll out the dough to about 1cm (½in) thickness and cut into rounds with the scone cutter. Place a teaspoon of marmalade in the centre of each round. Gather up the dough around the marmalade and pinch the edges together.
4. Place pinched-side-down on the greased baking tin, mark lightly with a cross, brush with milk or egg and sprinkle with granulated sugar.
5. Bake in the preheated oven for 15–20 minutes or until golden brown all over.

ICA Tip

The better the marmalade you use, the better the final result. Your local county market or farmers' market can be a great place to pick up quality preserves, or a well-stocked supermarket should have a good choice.

Chapter 7
Traybakes, Desserts & Puddings

Chocolate Biscuit Cake

MARY O'HALLORAN, CLOONEY QUIN GUILD, CLARE

My mother showed me how to make this moreish cake at a very young age. She would leave it in a cool room to set, and would often return to find just the centre remaining, the edges haven been picked away by small fingers. To this day we still make this cake for special family occasions.

Makes 16 generous squares

- 400g (14oz) Marietta biscuits
- 170g (6oz) butter
- 170g (6oz) caster sugar
- 4 tablespoons cocoa powder
- 1 egg, at room temperature, beaten

what you'll need

- baking tray
- baking parchment
- tinfoil or cling film

ICA Tip

You can add a handful of pitted dates or sultanas with the broken biscuits to give your biscuit cake a nice chewiness, while Maltesers add extra flavour as well as texture.

1. Line a baking tray with baking parchment. Roughly break up the biscuits into small pieces and set aside.

2. In a saucepan, melt the butter and sugar together over a medium heat for about 6–7 minutes, stirring constantly until the sugar has fully dissolved.

3. Remove from the heat, add the cocoa powder and beaten egg and keep stirring for two to three minutes to very gently cook out the eggs until the mixture comes together.

4. Add the broken biscuits and stir gently, ensuring the chocolate mixture coats all the biscuits.

5. Transfer to the prepared tray and push the mixture down, ensuring that it is nicely compacted. Cover well with foil or cling film and refrigerate for 4–6 hours to set. Allow to come to room temperature before cutting into squares.

Coconut Crunch Traybake

NOELINE POWER, TRAMORE GUILD, WATERFORD

The jam and coconut meringue topping make this traybake extra special, with lots of textures to bite through. This is a version of a recipe that my mother used to make, which had a very crunchy, crumbly base (see tip). The version below treats the same ingredients like a pastry – you could try either.

Makes 18 large squares

- 285g (10oz) plain flour, plus extra for dusting
- 110g (4oz) margarine
- 50g (2oz) caster sugar
- 3 egg yolks, beaten

for the topping

- 5 tablespoons (150g/5½oz) raspberry jam
- 3 egg whites
- 110g (4oz) caster sugar
- 110g (4oz) desiccated coconut

what you'll need

- Swiss roll tin, about 23cm x 33cm (9in x 13in)
- baking parchment
- rolling pin
- electric whisk (optional but recommended)

1. Preheat oven to 180°C/350°F/Gas 4. Line a Swiss roll tin with baking parchment so that it comes over the edges by about 7½cm (3in).

2. Sieve the flour into a large mixing bowl, then rub in the margarine with your fingers until you have a crumb-like texture. Mix in the sugar, then add the beaten egg yolks and two tablespoons of cold water and use a knife to work it into a dough; it should be soft, but not sticky.

3. Turn this out onto a lightly floured surface and roll it lightly with a rolling pin to fit the base of the tin. Place the pastry into the prepared Swiss roll tin.

4. To make the topping, loosen the raspberry jam with a little hot water for a spreadable consistency, and spread this on the pastry base. Beat the egg whites into stiff peaks, then gradually whisk in the sugar little by little. Finally fold in the coconut. Spread this mixture on top of the jam-covered base and bake in the preheated oven for 45 minutes.

5. Remove from the oven and allow to cool in the tray before cutting into 18 squares of approximately 5cm x 5cm (2in x 2in).

ICA Tip

For a crunchier base, cream the margarine and sugar together in a large mixing bowl, then gradually add the egg yolks and flour along with a little water to bring it together. Press this crumble into the base of the tin and top with jam and meringue.

Date and Almond Brownies

BREEGE LENIHAN, BALLINODE GUILD, MONAGHAN

Free from gluten and processed sugar, these rich brownies are naturally sweetened with dates for a guilt-free treat to share over a cuppa with family and friends. I like to bake them but you also have the option of omitting the baking soda and forming the mixture into no-bake brownie balls which you can pop onto lollipop sticks for a fun presentation.

Makes 16 squares

- 2 tablespoons milled linseed (flax)
- 140g (5oz) pitted Medjool dates
- 2 tablespoons maple syrup or honey
- 80ml full-fat coconut milk
- 60g (2½oz) almond butter (or peanut butter)
- 50g (2oz) coconut oil, melted, plus a little extra for greasing
- 200g (7oz) ground almonds
- 50g (2oz) raw cacao powder or cocoa powder
- ½ teaspoon bicarbonate of soda
- ¼ teaspoon salt
- 2 teaspoons vanilla extract
- 60g chopped nuts, such as walnuts, or dark chocolate chips (optional)

to finish

- cacao or cocoa powder, for dusting (optional)

what you'll need

- non-stick 20cm (8in) square baking tin or silicon tray
- food processor
- spatula

1. Preheat oven to 180°C/350°F/Gas 4. Grease a non-stick 20cm (8in) square baking tin or silicon tray with a little coconut oil.
2. Whisk the milled linseed in about six tablespoons (90ml/3fl oz) water and set aside for 10 minutes.
3. Blend the dates to a smooth paste in a food processor, checking for stones as you add them.
4. Add the maple syrup or honey along with the coconut milk, nut butter and linseed and water mixture. Combine well in the processor before blending in the melted coconut oil.
5. Add the ground almonds, cacao/cocoa powder, soda, salt and vanilla extract and blend for a minute before pulsing in the nuts or chocolate, if using.
6. Press the mixture into the prepared tray or tin, spreading evenly with a spatula. Bake in the preheated oven for 25–30 minutes.
7. Allow to cool in the tray or tin before slicing into 16 squares and dust with a little extra cacao or cocoa powder, if using. Store in an airtight container where they will keep well for a few days if refrigerated or for a month if frozen.

ICA Tip

Medjool dates can be difficult to source and pricey, but don't need soaking. If substituting with other pitted dates, pre-soak them in a little boiling water for 15 minutes and drain before blitzing.

Nutty Flake Fingers

SARAH MCDERMOTT, BALLINODE GUILD, SLIGO

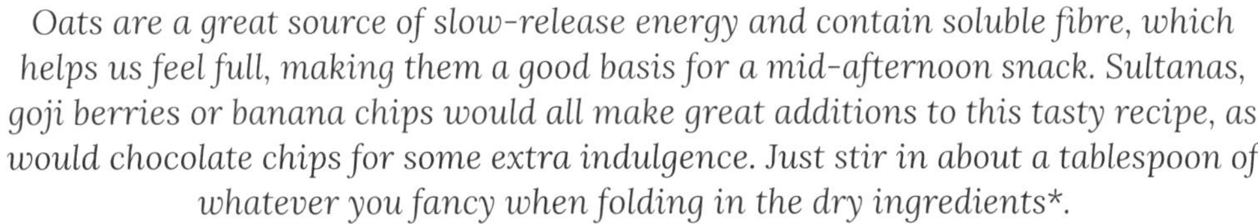

Oats are a great source of slow-release energy and contain soluble fibre, which helps us feel full, making them a good basis for a mid-afternoon snack. Sultanas, goji berries or banana chips would all make great additions to this tasty recipe, as would chocolate chips for some extra indulgence. Just stir in about a tablespoon of whatever you fancy when folding in the dry ingredients.*

Makes 12 fingers

- 1½ tablespoons golden syrup
- 170g (6oz) margarine
- 250g (9oz) porridge oats
- 170g (6oz) brown sugar
- 50g (2oz) chopped nuts (optional)
- 40g (1½oz) plain flour
- ¼ teaspoon salt

to finish

- 100g chocolate, melted (optional)

what you'll need

- Swiss roll tin, about 23cm x 33cm (9in x 13in)
- baking parchment
- heatproof bowl for bain marie or microwave
- wire rack

1. Preheat oven to 180°C/350°F/Gas 4. Lightly grease a Swiss roll tin or line with parchment.
2. Melt the syrup and margarine together in a bain marie (a large heatproof bowl set over a saucepan of simmering water). Fold the dry ingredients (oats, sugar, nuts, flour and salt) into the syrup mixture and mix well to incorporate*.
3. Pour the mixture into the prepared tin. Bake in the preheated oven for 15 minutes or until lightly golden.
4. Meanwhile melt the chocolate, if using: this can be done either in the bain marie or in a bowl in the microwave.
5. Remove the traybake from the oven and leave the tin on a wire rack to cool slightly before covering with melted chocolate. Cut into 12 fingers, or 24 bite-sized squares if you prefer.
6. Store in an airtight container where they will keep well for about a week.

'Whirly Gigs' Coffee Roll

NORA MCKINNEY, TAUGHBOYNE GUILD, DONEGAL

This oven-free recipe is very popular in our house and indeed with friends and neighbours. My grandchildren renamed it 'Whirly Gigs' as it reminds them of the little windmills that they played with as children. It is rather sweet, so a little goes a long way.

Makes two 20cm (8in) rolls

for the butter icing
- 85g (3oz) softened butter
- 85g (3oz) icing sugar

for the base
- 225g (8oz) digestive biscuits
- 170g (6oz) sweetened condensed milk
- 2 tablespoons coffee essence (see tip)
- 50g (2oz) ground almonds
- 50g (2oz) icing sugar

to finish
- 100g (3½oz) chocolate, melted

what you'll need
- blender or food processor (optional)
- rolling pin
- heatproof bowl for bain marie or microwave

1. In a small bowl, cream together the softened butter and icing sugar to make a butter icing. Set aside.

2. Crush the biscuits, either by pulsing in a food processor or blender or by placing in a Ziploc bag or tea towel and rolling with a rolling pin. In a large mixing bowl, combine the crushed biscuits with the condensed milk, coffee essence and ground almonds. Sieve in the icing sugar and stir well to incorporate fully.

3. Use dampened hands to form the mixture into a long roll. Cut this in half and then use a dampened rolling pin to roll each half out to an even square of approximately 20cm x 20cm (8in x 8in). Spread the butter icing evenly over each half, and carefully roll each up to resemble a Swiss roll.

4. Melt the chocolate either in a microwave or in a bain marie (a bowl set over a pot of simmering water) and top each roll with a little melted chocolate. Cut each roll into about 12 slices to serve.

ICA Tip

If you don't have coffee essence, you could use a tablespoon of strong coffee or espresso in its place, or dissolve two teaspoons of good instant coffee into equal parts hot water.

Versatile Almond Traybake

COLLETTE DALTON, SPA FENIT GUILD, KERRY

I have been using this recipe now for more years than I care to remember. It is practically foolproof and requires very little in the line of equipment. The filling can vary according to the season: homemade mincemeat at Christmas, marmalade in January or seasonal fruit jam later in the year.

Serves 10 as dessert, or makes 16 fingers or small squares

for the pastry base

- 110g (4oz) cold butter, cubed
- 25g (1oz) lard
- 225g (8oz) plain flour
- 2 tablespoons cold water

for the topping

- 225g (8oz) butter
- 225g (8oz) caster sugar
- 110g (4oz) ground rice or semolina
- 50g (2oz) ground almonds
- 50g (2oz) self-raising flour
- 2 eggs
- 10ml (⅔fl oz) almond extract or essence

for the filling

- 225g (8oz, or approx. half a jar) apricot or raspberry jam, marmalade or mincemeat

what you'll need

- 20cm x 28cm (8in x 11in) baking tray, lightly greased
- tinfoil or baking parchment
- rolling pin

1. Lightly grease a baking tray.
2. To make the pastry, rub the butter and lard into the flour until it resembles breadcrumbs. Add water gradually to bring together into a dough and knead gently. Shape into a disc shape, wrap in foil or parchment and refrigerate for 30 minutes while you make the topping. Preheat oven to 200°C/400°F/Gas 6.
3. Melt the butter in a saucepan, add the sugar and stir well for about 5–7 minutes or until the sugar and butter have both melted and combined. Add the ground rice or semolina, ground almonds and flour and mix well. Beat in the eggs with the almond extract and mix to incorporate fully. Set aside to cool.
4. Meanwhile, roll out the chilled pastry to fit the prepared baking tray. Press down into the edges, prick the base with a fork and line with baking parchment. Bake blind in the preheated oven for 10 minutes.
5. Remove from the oven and remove parchment. Spread with your filling of choice. Spread the topping mixture over this filling and return to the oven to bake for another 40–45 minutes or until golden brown.
6. Remove from the oven and allow to cool before cutting into your preferred size – fingers are perfect with a cup of tea or you could serve larger, dessert-sized pieces with custard or fresh cream. This traybake also freezes very well.

ICA *Tip*

As with all traybakes, if you line the inside of the tray with baking parchment so that it is coming over the edge, it will be easier to remove from the tin and divide up once baked.

Apple Crumble

MAUREEN ROBINSON, HORSELEAP STREAMSTOWN GUILD, WESTMEATH

Maureen has just celebrated her eightieth birthday, and her apple crumble is as popular with the next generation as it was with herself and her husband John's own growing family of 13 children. Quick and easy to prepare but resulting in a juicy flavourful base and crispy crumb, it is ideal for our modern lifestyles. If you want to put a smile on someone's face, give this crumble a go!

Serves 6–8

- 6 medium-sized cooking apples
- 60ml (2fl oz) water
- 85g (3oz) caster sugar
- 85g (3oz) brown sugar
- ¼ teaspoon ground cloves
- ¼ teaspoon ground nutmeg (or mixed spice)

for the topping

- 50g (2oz) plain flour
- 50g (2oz) wheaten meal
- 50g (2oz) porridge oats
- 85g (3oz) butter, room temperature
- 85g (3oz) brown sugar, plus a little extra to finish
- a drizzle of honey

to serve (optional)

- custard, ice-cream, fresh cream or crème fraîche

what you'll need

- ovenproof glass, pyrex or ceramic dish

1. Preheat oven to 190°C/375°F/Gas 5.

2. Peel, core and slice the apples. Scatter them into the base of an ovenproof dish together with the water, caster and brown sugars and ground cloves and nutmeg. Toss to coat the apple well.

3. To make the topping, combine the flour, wheaten meal and oats in a bowl. Cut the butter into pieces and rub it into the flour mixture to form a crumble. Mix in the sugar to combine, then stir in the honey.

4. Transfer this mixture onto the apples and dust the top with a little extra brown sugar.

5. Bake in the preheated oven for about 45 minutes or until golden brown. Serve hot with your choice of custard, ice-cream, fresh cream or crème fraîche.

ICA Tip

Try swapping the apple for pear or plums – or indeed whatever fresh seasonal fruit you fancy or happen to have a glut of.

Apple and Blueberry Pudding

ASTRID MOFFETT, BALLYBAY GUILD, MONAGHAN

This is a traditional recipe that my dad's mother used; then my mother used it and now I use it. The original recipe would have been made at harvest time when there were abundant blackberries and other harvest fruits. I use blueberries as they are very popular but you can use any fruits that you like in this recipe, though I do feel that tinned fruit is too soft and will burn. Be inventive and enjoy.

Serves 8

- 4 cooking apples, stewed in a little water (or shop-bought if you prefer)
- 225g (8oz) butter (softened) or margarine
- 225g (8oz) caster sugar
- 225g (8oz) self-raising flour
- 1 teaspoon baking powder
- 4 large eggs
- 30ml (1fl oz) sunflower oil
- 125g (4½oz) fresh blueberries

to serve

- 1–2 tablespoons caster sugar, for sprinkling
- cream or custard

what you'll need

- 23cm (9in) pie dish
- spatula

1. Preheat oven to 190°C/375°F/Gas 5. Generously grease a 23cm (9in) pie dish. To stew the apples (if not using shop-bought), peel, core and slice the apples and stew in a couple of tablespoons of water for 8–10 minutes until softened. Set aside to cool.

2. Beat the butter or margarine and sugar together in a large mixing bowl until creamy and light. Sieve the flour and baking powder into a separate mixing bowl.

3. Add the eggs one at a time to the butter-sugar mixture, together with about two teaspoons of sunflower oil, mixing in well before the next addition of egg and oil. Once everything is incorporated, fold in the sieved flour to create a soft batter.

4. Transfer the mixture into the greased pie dish and use a spatula to spread well. Loosely spread over the stewed apple to cover the top of the cake. Scatter over the blueberries.

5. Bake in the preheated oven for 45–60 minutes until well set. Remove from oven and sprinkle with sugar when hot. Serve with cream or custard.

ICA *Tip*

If you'd like to layer in some extra flavour, consider adding a few drops of vanilla extract or ½ teaspoon of ground spice such as nutmeg or cinnamon to the stewed apple.

Salem Snow Pudding

KATHLEEN MURRAY, FRENCHPARK GUILD, ROSCOMMON

Like many of her generation, my late mother emigrated to the USA where she and her young friends from all over Ireland worked for rich Americans in their homes in Salem, Massachusetts. Her job was looking after two children. A friend who trained as a cook gave her this recipe for a cold summer pudding, which she later made for her own children. The lengthy whisking time requires a bit of patience, but a stand mixer and electric whisk will make this less arduous.

Serves 8–10

- 5 leaves of gelatine
- 170g (6oz) caster sugar
- 275ml (½ pint) boiling water
- juice and zest of 1 large lemon
- 3 large egg whites

for the custard

- 570ml (1 pint) full-fat milk
- 4–5 lemon balm leaves (optional; and see tip)
- 85g (3oz) caster sugar
- 3 large egg yolks

what you'll need

- stand mixer (optional but recommended)
- electric whisk (optional but recommended)
- strainer (if using lemon balm)

ICA *Tip*

You could use lavender or even rosemary in place of the lemon balm, but only a little of whatever herb you add, in order to create a subtle flavour.

1. Fully submerge the gelatine leaves in a shallow bowl of cold water for five minutes. Meanwhile, in a large mixing bowl, dissolve the sugar in the boiling water together with the lemon juice and zest, stirring until fully dissolved.

2. While the lemon mixture is still hot, remove the gelatine from the cold water, squeeze it out and place it into the sugar water mixture. Keep stirring to melt the gelatine. Allow to cool at room temperature and then refrigerate for 30–40 minutes to semi-set and thicken.

3. Beat the cooled gelatine mixture in a stand mixer until it is stiff and very frothy, about 15 minutes. In a separate, clean bowl, beat the egg whites with an electric whisk until they hold soft peaks, about five minutes. Gently fold these whites into the gelatine mixture and beat for another five minutes until tripled in volume. Transfer to a large serving bowl and refrigerate for about three hours to set.

4. To make the custard, heat the milk gently along with any flavourings, if using. Add the sugar and stir to dissolve fully. Beat the egg yolks in a medium bowl.

5. Pour the sweetened milk slowly into the beaten egg yolks (through a strainer to remove the herbs, if using). Whisk well before returning to the saucepan. Cook gently, stirring continually and taking care to prevent the custard from reaching boiling point. If it shows any sign of curdling, turn very quickly into a cold bowl and whisk briskly.

6. Once the custard has reached a consistency that thinly coats a wooden spoon, set it aside to cool in the saucepan. Cover with a lid to avoid skin forming while cooling. Serve both the pudding and custard cold.

Grand-da Kavanagh's Upside-down Rhubarb Treat

CONNIE MCEVOY, TERMONFECKIN GUILD, LOUTH

Two stools of rhubarb in my garden provide me with fresh fillings for pies, tarts and stews annually from February until October – and later, thanks to my freezer. When I decide to have Grand-da's rhubarb treat, I bake it in my Aga, usually adding either fraughans (bilberries) or wild strawberries. Grand-ma told me years later that this recipe was a concocted version of a scone mixture (see page 144 for the full story) and that a white soda currant dough could just as easily be used.

Serves 12

- 225g (8oz) plain flour
- 2 heaped teaspoons baking powder
- a pinch of salt
- 25g (1oz) brown sugar
- 50g (2oz) butter, cubed
- 1 egg, beaten
- 100ml (3½fl oz) milk
- 2–3 tablespoons Bailey's Irish Cream

for the fruit filling

- 1½lb/675g rhubarb
- 110g (4oz) brown sugar
- 1–2 handfuls of fraughans (wild bilberries), wild strawberries or blueberries (optional)

what you'll need

- 25cm (10in) round cake tin or Pyrex casserole dish
- rolling pin
- palette knife

ICA Tip

The dough can also be used to make Bailey's scones – add another 25g (1oz) of flour to make the dough more manageable. Kirsch, Cointreau or brandy will work well in place of Bailey's Irish Cream.

1. Preheat oven to 200°C/400°F/Gas 6. Grease a 25cm (10in) round cake tin or Pyrex casserole dish.
2. Wash the rhubarb well, chop it into uniform chunks of about 5cm (2in) and set aside.
3. Sieve the flour, baking powder and salt into a large mixing bowl. Stir in the brown sugar. Rub the butter into the flour mixture with your fingers until you have a crumb-like texture.
4. Whisk the egg in a mug or small bowl with a fork, add the milk and Bailey's and whisk again. Make a well in the dry ingredients, pour all of the liquid in at once and mix to a soft dough.
5. Turn out onto a flour-dusted board and roll to required size to fit the cake tin or casserole dish. Fill the base of the tin or dish with the rhubarb and scatter over the brown sugar (and berries, if using). Top with the dough lid, tucking it in at the sides.
6. Bake in the preheated oven for 25–35 minutes or until the top is crispy and golden brown and the fruit is juicy and soft.
7. Remove from the oven and allow to cool a little in the tin or dish before carefully turning it out upside-down onto a serving platter, loosening the sides first with a palette knife. Alternatively, leave in the tin or dish and simply cut into portions to lift out individually to serve.

Grand-da Kavanagh's Rhubarb

CONNIE MCEVOY, TERMONFECKIN GUILD, LOUTH

As a five-year-old child, I was used to seeing my mother bake wheaten, white soda and currant bread on a daily basis in a bastible (pot oven) over an open fire. On Saturdays she would bake apple or rhubarb tarts, in case of unannounced visitors on Sunday afternoons. I was often tasked with operating the fanners for the duration in order to maintain the fire at the desired temperature and inform her if the hot cinders on the lid were turning grey and needed to be replaced with some hot firing.

I never knew that other goodies could be produced over an open fire until I was marooned on my grandparents' farm from 10 January until 19 March due to the snow of 1947. Grand-ma Kavanagh and Aunt Peg did most of the cooking and baking for the seven adults and me, but Grand-da would often rustle up something for suppertime, which was always eaten around 6p.m.

An avid gardener, he was very proud of his crop of rhubarb, which had been treated with a generous helping of horse manure, covered with straw and forced for early cutting by placing old bottomless buckets on top during the autumn of 1946.

Grand-da surprised us all on the last day of February when he arrived into the kitchen with an armful of rhubarb, announcing that he was going to give us all a great treat for supper that evening. After washing and chopping the rhubarb, he fixed a sheet of butter paper in the small pot oven and sprinkled some flour over it. I watched carefully as he then tipped in the prepared rhubarb and shook some dark brown sugar over it. Next he sifted flour and baking powder into a bowl, to which he added brown sugar. He cut a small skelp of farmer's butter off the block, cut it in small pieces and rubbed it into the flour mixture. Taking a mug from the dresser he whisked an egg with a fork and added some milk and a drop of brandy. Nothing was weighed or measured, but after spilling this mixture into the bowl he formed a ball of dough that he was happy with and placed and shaped it to fit on top of the rhubarb in the pot oven before baking over the open fire.

After a while he decreed that his rhubarb treat was ready: all adults were in agreement (judging by the aroma that was wafting through the kitchen) so he placed in front of the fireplace a large delph meat platter that had juice veins and a well. He removed the oven lid and tilted his supper treat onto it upside-down with a flick of his wrists. Aunt Peg served it to us with whipped cream that she had slightly sweetened with brown sugar. I still remember just how delicious that warm treat was. I make it often myself, using fresh rhubarb from my own garden.

See page 143 for the recipe for Grand-da Kavanagh's Upside-down Rhubarb Treat.

LAZY DAY BAKING • LAZY DAY •

Orange and Cranberry Pudding

HELEN KAVANAGH, BORRIS-IN-OSSORY GUILD, LAOIS

My mother Lily Sheeran, who has been an ICA member for more than 70 years, always made marmalade. When she got older my son David would go to her house to help her squeeze the oranges and lift the pots onto the cooker. David still makes marmalade on a regular basis, using his nana's recipe and supplying all his family and friends. This steamed pudding recipe was inspired by his homemade variety.

Serves 6–8

- 170g (6oz) fine breadcrumbs (grated or blitzed in a food processor)
- 110g (4oz) caster sugar
- 85g (3oz) self-raising flour, sieved
- 170g (6oz) margarine, plus a little extra for greasing
- 2 eggs, beaten
- juice and zest of 1 orange
- 110g (4oz) cranberries, fresh or frozen
- 80ml (3fl oz) semi-skimmed milk
- 8 tablespoons (200g/7oz) marmalade

to serve

- custard, cream or ice-cream

what you'll need

- 1 large ovenproof pudding bowl (or two smaller)
- food processor (optional)
- greaseproof paper
- tinfoil
- string or twine
- saucer
- roasting tin

1. Preheat oven to 180°C/350°F/Gas 4. Grease a large pudding bowl (or two small bowls, one for freezing if you prefer) with a little margarine.

2. Mix the breadcrumbs together with the sugar and flour in a large mixing bowl, then rub the margarine into the mixture. Add the beaten eggs and orange juice and zest, then stir in the cranberries and milk along with three-quarters of the marmalade.

3. Spoon the remaining marmalade into the greased bowl, spreading well to cover the base (this will form a topping; it should drizzle down the sides when the pudding is turned out). Pour the pudding mixture into the bowl and smooth the top with the back of a spoon.

4. Cover the top with a circle of greaseproof paper to fit the bowl, then measure out a larger piece of greaseproof paper, lay a piece of tinfoil over it and fold a pleat in the centre of the paper and foil to allow the pudding room to expand. Place these over the top of the pudding bowl and tie tightly in place with string or twine. (You can use an extra piece of string or twine to tie on a handle, to make it easy to remove.)

5. Place the pudding bowl on a saucer in a roasting tin which has been half filled with hot water. Lay out a very large piece of tinfoil flat on the worktop. Place the roasting tin on the tinfoil and wrap to make a parcel, completely enclosing the tin within the foil. Transfer carefully to the preheated oven to steam for 2½ hours. (The pudding could alternatively be steamed stovetop but oven steaming offers the advantage of a steam-free kitchen and frees you from having to top up the water as it boils dry.)

6. Remove carefully from the oven and leave to cool slightly before turning it out onto a plate and serving warm with custard, cream or ice-cream.

Gooey Chocolate Pudding

CATHERINE O'DOWD, MONAGHAN TOWN GUILD, MONAGHAN

Served warm so it is still molten in the middle, this is the nicest chocolate pudding ever, and very easy to prepare. My daughter makes it all the time and it's a firm family favourite.

Serves 6–8

- 250g (9oz) good-quality chocolate
- 250g (9oz) butter
- 200g (7oz) caster sugar
- 4 eggs
- 70g (2½oz) self-raising flour

to serve

- whipped cream or ice-cream

what you'll need

- 20cm (8in) round springform tin or ovenproof baking dish
- baking parchment or greaseproof paper
- heatproof bowl for bain marie or microwave
- electric whisk (optional)

ICA Tip

Use the best quality chocolate you can afford – it really will make all the difference. You can add some fresh raspberries or white chocolate chunks after folding in the flour to change things up a bit.

1. Preheat oven to 180°C/350°F/Gas 4. Line a 20cm (8in) round springform tin with baking parchment or greaseproof paper. Alternatively, grease an ovenproof dish.

2. Melt the chocolate, stirring periodically to ensure that there are no solid chunks: this can be done either in a bowl in the microwave or in a bain marie (a heatproof bowl placed over a pot of simmering water). Set aside to cool off a little.

3. Melt the butter and mix it into the sugar in a large mixing bowl, whisking until light and fluffy. Whisk in the eggs one at a time, incorporating each one fully before adding the next.

4. Once the chocolate has cooled a little, fold it into the egg mixture a little a time with a wooden spoon. Fold in the flour, taking care not to overmix and knock out the air.

5. Pour the mixture into the lined tin and bake in the preheated oven for 25 minutes or until there is only a slight wobble left in the centre. If baking in an ovenproof dish, it will take about 20 minutes.

6. Remove from the oven and allow to cool a little before carefully removing from the tin. Serve warm, cut into gooey slices and perhaps with some whipped cream or ice-cream to accompany it. Alternatively, if using an ovenproof dish, you could serve it family-style and allow people to scoop out helpings at the table.

Pavlova

JOAN MCLOUGHLIN, CAPPAMORE GUILD, LIMERICK

Pavlova is such a treat with its contrast of crispy shell and that gorgeously gooey centre, topped with whipped cream and whatever fresh fruit you fancy. Berries like strawberries or raspberries, tropical fruits like pineapple or kiwi fruit and stone fruits like peaches or plums are all particularly good.

Serves 8–10

- 7 egg whites
- 400g (14oz) caster sugar
- 2 drops vanilla extract
- 6 teaspoons cornflour
- 3 teaspoons white wine vinegar

to serve

- 400ml (¾ pint) fresh cream
- fresh ripe fruit of choice

what you'll need

- ovenproof square dish of 25cm x 25cm (10in x 10in)
- handheld electric whisk or stand mixer
- spatula

ICA Tip

Consider making homemade mayonnaise with those leftover egg yolks; it requires a bit of patience but other than that it's surprisingly easy.

1. Preheat oven to 130°C/250°F/Gas ½. Check that your ovenproof square dish is very clean and dry.

2. In a large and very clean bowl, whisk the egg whites with half of the sugar until it forms stiff peaks.

3. Reduce the speed of the whisk or mixer and continue to whisk as you add the remaining sugar and the vanilla extract, cornflour and vinegar.

4. Pour the mixture into the square dish and bake in the preheated oven for 80 minutes or until the shell is nice and crisp. Remove from the oven and leave to cool fully. This will keep well for a day or two in an airtight container so can be made in advance and then dressed at the last minute before serving.

5. To serve, whip the cream and spread across the pavlova with a spatula, and then decorate with fresh fruit of your choice.

LAZY DAY BAKING • LAZY DAY •

Swiss Nut Torte

MARY J. GALLAGHER, BONNICONLON GUILD, MAYO

You don't need to be a professional baker to make this beautiful torte. Whenever I have somebody calling, it is always top of my list to serve either as a teatime treat or dessert. It is quite unusual and people often ask me for the recipe.

Serves 8–12

- 85g (3oz) softened butter
- 310g (11oz) plain flour
- 110g (4oz) caster sugar
- ½ teaspoon salt
- 1 egg
- 2 teaspoons rum
- zest of 1 lemon

for the filling

- 170g (6oz) caster sugar
- 275ml (½ pint) whipping cream, room temperature
- 3 tablespoons honey
- 2 tablespoons kirsch or brandy
- 350g (12oz) walnuts (or pecans, if you prefer)

to glaze

- 1 egg yolk, lightly beaten
- 1 tablespoon milk

what you'll need

- tall 23cm (9in) springform cake tin
- baking sheet
- baking parchment
- rolling pin
- wire rack

ICA Tip

It is important to use a cake tin for this recipe, as the higher walls are needed to hold in all the liquid.

1. Preheat oven to 190°C/350°F/Gas 4. Lightly grease a tall 23cm (9in) springform cake tin and line a baking sheet with parchment.

2. In a large mixing bowl, beat the butter until fluffy. Mix the flour with the sugar and salt, add to the butter and beat until crumbly. In a small bowl, beat the egg and stir in the rum and lemon zest. Stir this into the large mixing bowl to moisten and bind the flour mixture into a dough.

3. Divide the dough into thirds and roll out to a shape and size in order to distribute as follows: one-third will cover the base of the springform tin; another third should form a wall on the sides of the tin to a height of 2.5cm (1in); and the remaining third should be rolled into a ½cm (¼in) thick rectangle and placed on the lined baking sheet. Cover and chill this crust and rolled dough (in the tin) for 30 minutes.

4. To make the filling, melt the sugar in a saucepan over a low heat, stirring constantly for about five minutes until golden and dissolved. Take care, as the sugar will become extremely hot. Remove from the heat and slowly (and carefully) stir in the cream to gently heat it and continue stirring until the sugar has dissolved completely. Add the honey and kirsch or brandy and finally stir in the nuts. Remove from the heat and set aside to cool for about five minutes before pouring the mixture inside the dough-lined tin taken from the fridge.

5. Cut the rectangle of dough (from the baking sheet) into strips of about ½cm (¼in) in width and layer these on top of the pie in a lattice design. Seal the edges of the crust by pressing with the prongs of a fork, and brush a mixture of beaten yolk and milk over the crust. Bake in the preheated oven for about 35–40 minutes or until set and golden all over.

6. Remove from the oven and leave in the tin on a wire rack to cool fully before releasing the springform tin and carefully removing the torte. Divide into about 12 portions if serving as a dessert, or about 8 portions for a teatime treat.

Chapter 8
Cakes for Every Occasion

QUICK & EASY • & • QUICK & EASY

Apple, Date and Walnut Cake

EILEEN REDMOND, CAMROSS GUILD, WEXFORD

I love to make this cake in autumn, when we have our own apples and walnuts from the trees in the garden. I sometimes use no-soak prunes or apricots instead of dates, but the dates really are my favourite.

Serves 10–12

- 110g (4oz) butter, softened
- 175g (6oz) soft dark brown sugar
- 110g (4oz) self-raising flour
- ½ teaspoon baking powder
- 110g (4oz) wheaten meal
- 2 eggs
- 3–4 tablespoons milk
- 1 cooking apple, peeled, cored and roughly chopped
- 85g (3oz) pitted dates, chopped
- 110g (4oz) walnuts, chopped

what you'll need

- 900g (2lb) loaf tin
- wire rack

1. Preheat oven to 180°C/350°F/Gas 4. Grease a 900g (2lb) loaf tin.
2. Cream the butter and sugar in a large mixing bowl until light and fluffy. Sieve the self-raising flour and baking powder together into a separate bowl and fold in the wheaten meal. In a third bowl, whisk the eggs and milk together.
3. Add a third of the flour mixture to the creamed butter, mixing to incorporate before adding a third of the egg mixture. Repeat twice to incorporate both mixtures gradually, then stir in the fruit and nuts.
4. Transfer the mixture to the prepared tin and bake in the preheated oven for about 60–65 minutes or until it feels springy to touch and a skewer inserted into the centre comes out clean.
5. Remove from the oven and allow to cool in the tin for about 5–10 minutes before turning out onto a wire rack to cool fully.

French Apple Cake with Mascarpone Icing

PATRICIA CAVANAGH, BALLINODE GUILD, MONAGHAN

My son lives in Barcelona with his Parisian girlfriend Valèrie Aubrey. She loves cooking and baking, and this lovely soft apple cake is one of her recipes. It reminds me of the apple cake my mother used to make; I sometimes add a pinch of cinnamon or nutmeg to give it a bit of an Irish twist.

Serves 10

- 50g (2oz) butter
- 4 crisp, sweet apples such as Royal Gala
- juice of ½ lemon
- 6 eggs (2 whole, 4 yolk only)
- 400ml (¾ pint) milk
- 300ml (10fl oz) sunflower oil
- 1½ teaspoons vanilla extract
- 400g (14oz) plain flour, plus extra for dusting
- 270g (9½oz) brown sugar
- 2 teaspoons baking powder
- 1 teaspoon salt

for the mascarpone icing (optional)

- 125g (4½oz) mascarpone
- 250g (9oz) icing sugar
- juice and zest of ½ orange

what you'll need

- 23cm–25cm (9in–10in) springform tin
- frying pan
- spatula

ICA Tip

For a speedier version of this delicious cake, skip the mascarpone icing and simply dust with a little sieved icing sugar – it is so rich and moist that it works on its own.

1. Preheat oven to 170°C/325°F/Gas 3. Grease the bottom and sides of the springform tin with half the butter and then sprinkle with flour.

2. Peel and cut the apples into bite-size pieces. Heat the rest of the butter in a frying pan over a medium heat and brown the apples for 5–10 minutes, until they are soft and starting to break down. Set aside in a bowl and pour over the lemon juice (to stop them turning brown), mixing well.

3. Beat two whole eggs in a large mixing bowl together with the milk, sunflower oil and vanilla extract and mix well. In another bowl, sieve three-quarters of the flour (reserving 100g/3½oz) and mix in the brown sugar, baking powder and salt. Fold these dry ingredients into the egg-milk mixture and combine all into a wet batter.

4. Divide this batter evenly between two bowls. Beat the egg yolks and add them to the first bowl, mixing well before gently incorporating the apple pieces. Sieve the remaining flour into the second bowl, and fold in to incorporate. Then gently pour this mixture into the prepared tin quickly followed by the mixture from the first bowl with the apple.

5. Bake in the preheated oven for about 60–75 minutes, or until a skewer inserted into the centre comes out clean. Remove from the oven and allow it cool for 10–20 minutes in the tin before turning it out carefully. Allow to cool fully.

6. To make the icing, beat the mascarpone cheese and icing sugar in a large mixing bowl, then slowly incorporate the orange juice and zest. Continue beating for about five minutes or until the cream is soft and firm. Refrigerate the icing until the cake is completely cool. Use a long spatula to cover the cake with the icing, and grate some orange zest on top.

Gort Apple Cake

JOSEPHINE HELLY, ICA NATIONAL PRESIDENT, GORT GUILD, GALWAY

This tasty apple cake is traditional to my part of Galway. It couldn't be simpler and if you use a jar of shop-bought apple purée, it can be thrown together in a few minutes from store-cupboard ingredients and popped into the oven while you enjoy a Sunday roast, or maybe before guests arrive for tea.

Serves 10–12

- 140g (5oz) margarine (or butter, softened)
- 140g (5oz) caster sugar, plus extra for dusting
- 2 eggs, beaten
- 225g (8oz) plain flour
- 1 level teaspoon bicarbonate of soda
- 1 level teaspoon ground cinnamon
- ½ level teaspoon ground ginger
- ½ level teaspoon mixed spice
- 110g (4oz) seeded raisins
- 110g (4oz) mixed currants and sultanas
- 35g (1½oz) candied peel
- grated rind of ½ lemon
- 60g (2½oz) walnuts, chopped
- 275ml (½ pint) apple purée, shop-bought or homemade (see below)

for the apple purée, if making

- 2 medium cooking apples
- 85g (3oz) soft light brown sugar

what you'll need

- 23cm (9in) cake tin
- blender or potato masher

1. Preheat oven to 150°C/300°F/Gas 2. Grease a 23cm (9in) cake tin.

2. To make the apple purée (if not using a shop-bought jar), peel, core and slice the apples and stew in a couple of tablespoons of water for about 10–12 minutes or until softened. Allow to cool a little and then blitz to a pulp in a blender, with a stick blender or with a potato masher. Add the brown sugar to taste and set aside to cool.

3. In a large mixing bowl, beat the margarine (or butter) and caster sugar to a cream. Add the beaten eggs gradually, incorporating each amount before adding the next.

4. Sieve the flour into a separate bowl together with the soda and spices, then fold this into the creamed sugar mixture. Finally, fold in the dried fruit, peel, grated lemon rind and chopped walnuts together with the apple purée. Blend the mixture well.

5. Turn the batter into the greased cake tin, dust with caster sugar and bake in the preheated oven for about 75–80 minutes.

6. Remove from the oven and leave to cool before removing from the tin.

Mulberry Crumble Cake

JANICE CASEY BRACKEN, ICA COOKERY SCHOOL, AN GRIANÁN

This fruity, crumbly cake is a tribute to the rich pickings from our fruit trees in An Grianán. Each summer multitudes of fruits and berries bloom in our garden, but my favourite of all is the mulberry – a sweet, tangy and juicy berry that looks like a long blackberry. As you come up the driveway, just as the house comes into view there is a magnificent mulberry tree on your right-hand side. We can often be found picking them on Sunday mornings in our weekend courses.

Serves 10

for the crumble topping

- 50g (2oz) plain flour
- 50g (2oz) ground almonds
- 50g (2oz) golden caster sugar
- 50g (2oz) cold butter, cubed
- ¼ teaspoon fresh thyme (or 1 teaspoon dried thyme)

for the cake batter

- 175g (6oz) softened butter
- 185g (6½oz) golden caster sugar
- 3 large eggs
- 225g (8oz) self-raising flour
- 1 teaspoon baking powder
- 85g (3oz) sour cream
- 100g (3½oz) ground almonds
- 250g (9oz) ripe mulberries or blackberries (about 1½ cups, washed and trimmed)
- 1 tablespoon cornflour (optional)

to serve

- icing sugar
- whipped fresh cream

what you'll need

- 20cm (8in) round loose-bottomed cake tin
- baking parchment
- stand mixer or electric whisk
- wire rack

1. Preheat oven to 180°C/350°F/Gas 4. Grease a 20cm (8in) round loose-bottomed cake tin and line with parchment.

2. For the crumble, sieve the flour into a mixing bowl and mix with the almonds and sugar, then rub in the butter with your fingers until you have a crumb-like texture. Mix in the thyme and set aside.

3. To make the cake batter, cream the butter and sugar together, then beat in the eggs. Sieve in half of the flour together with the baking powder, and fold it in to combine fully. Then stir in the sour cream followed by the rest of the sieved flour and the ground almonds. Beat with an electric whisk or in a stand mixer for about five minutes or until very smooth, ensuring no lumps remain.

4. Dust the berries very lightly in cornflour, to help prevent them sinking to the bottom of the cake during the baking process.

5. Pour the cake mix into the prepared cake tin and tap the tin to release any air pockets from the mixture. Place your dusted fruit on top, ensuring that they are evenly distributed. Scatter over the crumble mixture.

6. Bake on the middle shelf of the preheated oven for 50–65 minutes or until a skewer inserted into the centre comes out clean.

7. Remove from the oven and leave to cool in the tin for 15 minutes before transferring to a wire rack to cool fully. Serve with a dusting of icing sugar and a dollop of fresh cream. This cake will store well in an airtight container for up to two days.

Vegan Blackberry Cake

JANICE CASEY BRACKEN, ICA COOKERY SCHOOL, AN GRIANÁN

When taking a late summer evening stroll from An Grianán to the beach, with the brambles laden with berries, I love to collect fresh blackberries. I use them to make beautiful jams to remind me of those long summer evenings, even in the depths of winter, or transform them into comforting baked treats such as this moist vegan cake.

Serves 10

- 125g (4½oz) blackberries
- 1 tablespoon cornflour (optional)
- 225g (8oz) plain flour
- 1 teaspoon bicarbonate of soda
- a pinch of salt
- 240ml (8fl oz) oat milk
- 210g (7½oz) unrefined caster sugar
- 1 tablespoon lime juice
- 50ml (2fl oz) vegetable oil or coconut oil

for the icing

- 2 tablespoons lime juice
- zest of 1 lime
- 175g (6oz) vegan-friendly icing sugar

what you'll need

- 900g (2lb) loaf tin
- baking parchment
- electric whisk
- wire rack

ICA Tip

Keep an eye on the cake as it bakes; if the top starts to brown too quickly, cover it in baking parchment.

1. Preheat oven to 180°C/350°F/Gas 4. Grease a 900g (2lb) loaf tin and line with baking parchment.

2. Wash, dry and slice the berries. Set half aside for topping the cake later, and dust the rest lightly in cornflour (this will prevent them sinking into the batter during the baking).

3. Sieve the flour, soda and salt together into a bowl. In a separate large mixing bowl, combine the oat milk, sugar, lime juice and oil, and beat with an electric whisk until well mixed. Add the flour mixture a spoonful at a time, beating to fully incorporate into a smooth, airy batter with no lumps.

4. Pour this wet batter into the prepared loaf tin and place your dusted blackberries on top of the cake mix. Bake on the middle shelf of the preheated oven for 45–55 minutes or until a skewer inserted into the centre comes out clean (but avoid skewering the berries as they will be moist and sticky). Remove from the oven and leave to cool in the tin for 20 minutes before transferring to a wire rack to cool fully.

5. When the cake is completely cooled, mix together lime juice, zest and icing sugar until smooth and spoon onto top of the cake. Slice the reserved blackberries, scatter over and serve.

Lemon and Almond Cake

BREEGE LENIHAN, BALLINODE GUILD, MONAGHAN

This cake is lovely for a party, coffee morning or as a dessert with a little ice-cream and soft fruit. Using gluten-free baking powder makes the recipe fully gluten-free, but regular is fine, though be aware that some icing sugar is unsuitable for coeliacs. This can be made with lemons or oranges, depending on what you have to hand.

Serves 10

- 200g (7oz) softened butter, plus extra for greasing
- 200g (7oz) caster sugar
- 3 large eggs
- 250g (7oz) ground almonds
- 85g (3oz) fine polenta
- 1½ teaspoons gluten-free baking powder
- zest of 2 lemons or oranges

for the syrup

- juice of 2 lemons or oranges
- 100g (3½oz) icing sugar

what you'll need

- 23cm (9in) springform cake tin
- baking parchment
- stand mixer (or bowl and wooden spoon)
- wire rack
- skewer or toothpick

1. Preheat the oven to 180°C/gas mark 4/350°F. Lightly grease a 23cm (9in) springform cake tin and line the base with parchment.

2. Cream the butter and sugar together until pale and fluffy. Add one egg and beat until incorporated.

3. Combine the almonds, polenta and baking powder in a separate bowl, and beat a third of this into the butter-sugar-egg mixture, followed by another egg, then another third of the dry ingredients. Repeat with the final egg and remaining dry ingredients then add the citrus zest, beating well to fully incorporate.

4. Transfer the mixture to your prepared tin. Bake in the preheated oven for about 40 minutes or until it is golden and contracting slightly from the sides of the tin, at which point a skewer inserted into the centre of the cake should come out clean.

5. Meanwhile, to make the syrup, bring the citrus juice and icing sugar to a boil in a saucepan and remove immediately, stirring to dissolve the sugar.

6. Remove the cake from the oven and place the tin on a wire rack. Use a skewer or toothpick to make lots of little pricks in the top of the cake, pour over the warm syrup and leave to cool fully before removing from the tin.

ICA *Tip*

Some recipes call for unsalted butter but I often use ordinary salted butter. The syrup can be omitted if you want to cut down on sugar; it's not so moist and sweet but still very good.

Lemon Layer Cake

FRANCES MURRAY, BELTRA GUILD, SLIGO

This straightforward and easily achievable cake originated from an ICA booklet published in 1947, and was adapted by Maggie McMunn of the Beltra Guild from a recipe presented at a class given by home economics teacher Mrs Noone. You could make this into an orange layer cake by simply substituting grated orange rind and orange juice for the lemon.

Serves 6–8

- 110g (4oz) margarine
- 85g (3oz) granulated sugar
- grated rind and juice of ½ lemon
- 2 eggs, beaten well
- 1 tablespoon milk
- 140g (5oz) self-raising flour

for the filling

- 1 egg, beaten
- 110g (4oz) granulated sugar
- grated rind and strained juice of ½ lemon
- 25g (1oz) butter

to decorate

- 200g (3½oz) icing sugar
- 1–2 tablespoons strained lemon juice
- a handful of flaked almonds, lightly toasted in a dry pan

what you'll need

- 450g (1lb) loaf tin
- wire rack
- spatula or palette knife

1. Preheat oven to 180°C/350°F/Gas 4. Grease a 450g (1lb) loaf tin.
2. Beat the margarine and sugar to a soft cream in a large mixing bowl. Add the grated lemon rind and well-beaten eggs and beat until smooth.
3. Sieve in the flour, stir in the milk and gradually add the lemon juice.
4. Turn into the prepared tin and bake for 45–60 minutes in the preheated oven or until a skewer inserted into the centre comes out clean. Remove from the oven, allow to cool on a wire rack and set aside for 24 hours.
5. The next day, to make the filling, bring some water to the boil. Beat the egg in a heatproof mixing bowl. Add the sugar, grated lemon rind, lemon juice and butter and place the bowl over a pot of very hot water, stirring until the mixture becomes smooth and thick. Set aside to cool fully.
6. Once the filling is cold, carefully remove the cake from the tin and slice horizontally through the centre. Spread over the filling with a spatula or palette knife and then sandwich the two halves back together.
7. To make the icing, rub the icing the sugar through a sieve and gradually add enough strained lemon juice to form a thick paste, about a tablespoon or two.
8. Spread this icing onto the cake with a spatula or palette knife, before decorating with toasted flaked almonds.

Orange Chiffon Cake

CLAIRE ANN MCDONNELL, MONEYSTOWN GUILD, WICKLOW

This beautifully light cake benefits from all the airiness that whisked eggs bring to its structure. The cake itself is relatively straightforward to prepare, but the results can be seriously impressive – especially if you ice it and have a bit of fun with the decoration. It's a great option for a large party cake: simply triple the ingredients and bake in a 25cm (10in) tin, then slice in half horizontally and fill with a buttercream before topping with the satin icing (also tripled). It would work very well with lime or lemon instead of orange.

Makes one 20cm (8in) cake

- 175g (6oz) self-raising flour
- 110g (4oz) caster sugar
- 4–5 tablespoons sunflower oil
- 3 medium eggs
- juice and zest of 2 medium oranges

for the orange satin icing (recommended)

- 1 teaspoon melted butter
- 175g (6oz) icing sugar
- juice and zest of 1 medium orange

for the buttercream icing (optional)

- 225g (8oz) butter, softened
- 450g (1lb) icing sugar
- grated zest of 1 orange
- 3–4 tablespoons orange juice

1. Preheat oven to 180°C/350°F/Gas 4. Grease a 20cm (8in) sponge cake tin and line with baking parchment.

2. Sieve the flour into a large mixing bowl and mix in the sugar. Make a well in the centre and add the oil, two egg yolks, orange juice and zest in that order, and beat until smooth.

3. In a separate large, clean mixing bowl, whisk three egg whites until light, fluffy and forming stiff peaks. Carefully fold one-third of the whisked whites into the flour and egg batter, taking care not to lose too much air as you do. Repeat with the remaining two-thirds.

4. Pour the mixture into the lined tin and bake in the preheated oven for 60–70 minutes or until a skewer inserted into the centre comes out clean. Remove from the oven and leave on a wire rack to cool fully before carefully turning the cake out from the tin.

5. Meanwhile, make your choice of icing: we recommend the satin icing but you could substitute it with a buttercream if you prefer, or use both if making a large party cake (see above). For the satin icing, melt the butter in a bain marie (a heatproof bowl set over a pot of boiling water). Stir in the icing sugar, orange rind and juice and allow to heat

to decorate

- orange jellies, crystallised orange slices or dried orange zest

what you'll need

- 20cm (8in) sponge cake tin (or 25cm/10in tin for large party cake)
- baking parchment
- wire rack
- heatproof bowl for bain marie
- spatula or palette knife

ICA Tip

- Chiffon cakes are sometimes made in a tube pan for even cooking and to maintain structure in the cake batter while cooking. Banging the batter-filled pan several times before baking will help release larger air pockets.

very gently for about 10 minutes, stirring periodically. Remove from the heat and beat until creamy and a good spreading consistency; if it seems a little thin, add more icing sugar to achieve the correct consistency.

6. If making the buttercream, beat the butter in a large mixing bowl until soft, then add half of the icing sugar and beat until smooth before adding the rest and beating until creamy. Stir in the orange zest and juice.

7. Once the cake is fully cool, spread over the satin icing or buttercream with a spatula or palette knife. If you wish to decorate the top further, you can do so with orange jellies and/or crystallised orange slices. Alternatively, allow some orange zest to dry a little (to make it easier to handle) and then use a stencil to sprinkle it into a pattern.

Yoghurt Citrus Cake

ANNE ROWLANDS, FEDAMORE GUILD, LIMERICK

This easy-peasy recipe was given to me by an aunt. I like to use a small yoghurt container to measure out the other ingredients, as it makes it very easy to remember and means you don't have to bother weighing things out – but we've given you both options here.

Serves 12

- 125g (4½oz) natural yoghurt (1 small carton)
- 250g (9oz) caster sugar (2 cartons' worth)
- 260g (9½oz) self-raising flour (3 cartons' worth)
- 3 eggs, beaten
- 1 teaspoon vanilla extract
- grated rind and juice of 1 orange or lemon

to serve

- 180ml (6fl oz) freshly whipped cream
  or
  125g (4½oz) natural yoghurt

what you'll need

- 900g (2lb) loaf tin
- baking parchment
- wire rack

1. Preheat oven to 150°C/300°F/Gas 2. Grease a 900g (2lb) tin and line with baking parchment.
2. In a large mixing bowl, beat the yoghurt, sugar, flour and eggs together until smooth. Stir in the vanilla extract and citrus juice and rind, mixing well.
3. Pour into the prepared tin and bake in the preheated oven for about one hour or until a skewer inserted into the centre comes out clean.
4. Remove from the oven and leave in the tin to cool for a few minutes before transferring to a wire rack to cool fully.
5. Serve cool with some cream or yoghurt.

ICA Tip

This cake would be delicious topped with the satin icing or the buttercream from the Orange Chiffon Cake (see page 164).

Quick Orange Cake

JOAN NOONE, BLANCHARDSTOWN GUILD, DUBLIN

This recipe is adapted from a battered and well-loved old 1960's cookbook of my mother's, Home Baked Breads and Cakes *by Mary Norwak. I've tweaked it a little for ease of use. I often make a gluten-free version, simply by using a good gluten-free self-raising flour.*

Makes one 20cm (8in) round cake

- 110g (4oz) butter
- 225g (8oz) caster sugar
- juice of 2 oranges
- 2 eggs, beaten
- 225g (8oz) self-raising flour, sieved
- ¼ teaspoon salt

for the topping

- grated rind of 2 oranges
- 3 tablespoons granulated sugar

what you'll need

- 20cm (8in) deep round cake tin
- baking parchment
- stand mixer or electric whisk
- wire rack

ICA Tip

If you wanted to make this more elaborate, you could top it with the satin or buttercream icing from page 164.

1. Preheat oven to 180°C/350°F/Gas 4. Grease a 20cm (8in) deep round tin and line the base and sides with baking parchment.

2. Spread the orange rind for the topping out on a board or plate near the oven to dry out a little and make it easier to handle.

3. Melt the butter in a small saucepan or a microwave on a low heat. In a large mixing bowl or a stand mixer, if using, combine the melted butter with the sugar. Stir in the orange juice and beaten eggs. Sieve in the flour and salt and beat well until light and fluffy.

4. In a small bowl, mix the dried orange rind and sugar together for the topping.

5. Pour the cake batter into the prepared cake tin, sprinkle with the orange sugar topping, and bake in the preheated oven for 45–60 minutes or until a skewer inserted into the centre comes out clean.

6. Remove from the oven and allow to cool in the tin for at least 10 minutes before transferring to a wire rack to cool fully.

Coffee and Chocolate Cake

BREDA MCDONALD, MULLINAVAT GUILD, KILKENNY

This rich and delicious cake makes a wonderful celebration cake. If making it for a loved one, neighbour or friend, it's nice to tie a ribbon around the chocolate fingers, once they have been secured into place. It looks a picture and tastes even better. It's better to make this a day before you want to ice and serve it.

Serves 8–10

- 225g (8oz) butter, softened
- 225g (8oz) caster sugar
- 1 tablespoon coffee essence (see tip)
- 5 large eggs
- 250g (9oz) self-raising flour

for the coffee and chocolate icing

- 175g (6oz) butter, softened
- 350g (12oz) icing sugar
- 110g (4oz) dark chocolate
- 1 tablespoon coffee essence
- 1 tablespoon boiling water

to finish

- 125ml (4fl oz) strong coffee
- 350g (12oz) chocolate fingers
- 55g (2oz) dark chocolate
- 55g (2oz) white chocolate
- 125g (4½oz) punnet of fresh raspberries

1. Preheat oven to 170°C/325°F/Gas 3. Grease a deep 20cm (8in) cake tin and line with baking parchment.

2. In a large mixing bowl, cream the butter with the sugar until very light and fluffy. Add the coffee essence and mix well. Beat the eggs in a small bowl and add a third of this to the creamed butter, mixing to incorporate. Sieve in about a third of the flour and mix well. Repeat twice to gradually incorporate all the egg and flour.

3. Pour the mixture into the prepared cake tin and bake in the preheated oven for 45–50 minutes or until well set and a skewer inserted into the centre comes out clean.

4. Remove from the oven and leave in the tin on a wire rack to cool fully before turning out and removing the baking parchment. Ideally you should have the cake made the day before you require it, in which case cover it and leave it overnight before icing.

5. To make the icing (ideally the next day), cream the butter and icing sugar together in a large mixing bowl for at least four or five minutes until very light and fluffy. Meanwhile, melt the dark chocolate; this can be done either in a bowl in the microwave or in a bain marie (a heatproof bowl placed over a pot of simmering water). Add the melted chocolate, coffee essence and boiling water to the butter icing: the first two to flavour and colour the icing, and the latter to make the icing very soft and pliable.

what you'll need

- deep 20cm (8in) cake tin
- baking parchment
- sharp serrated knife
- wire rack
- heatproof bowl for bain marie or microwave
- pastry brush

ICA *Tip*

If you don't have coffee essence, you could use a tablespoon of strong coffee or espresso in its place, or dissolve two teaspoons of good instant coffee into equal parts hot water.

6. To assemble the cake, use a sharp serrated knife to split the sponge horizontally into three equal pieces. Brush a little of the strong coffee over each layer of the sponge to moisten. Spread some of the butter icing on top of each of the three layers of sponge, re-assemble the cake into its original format and cover the sides with the remaining butter icing. Carefully stick on the chocolate fingers vertically all the way around the sides of the cake. Coarsely grate the two types of chocolate over the top (don't grate it too finely or it will fall off when sliced) and decorate with fresh raspberries.

Chocolate Fudge Cake

RITA CAROLAN, CLONES GUILD, MONAGHAN

I have had this recipe for about 20 years. It has become a family favourite and is requested for all types of family occasions. Though it looks really impressive, it's surprisingly easy to make, because it's made with the all-in-one method.

Serves 8

- 185g (6½oz) plain flour
- 140g (5oz) caster sugar
- 2–3 teaspoons good quality cocoa powder
- 1½ level teaspoons baking powder
- 1½ level teaspoons bicarbonate of soda
- 2 eggs
- 150ml (¼ pint) milk
- 150ml (¼ pint) vegetable oil
- 1 tablespoon golden syrup

for the filling

- 110g (4oz) milk chocolate
- 110g (4oz) icing sugar
- 50g (2oz) cream cheese
- 50g (2oz) softened butter
- 2 tablespoons orange juice or Cointreau liqueur

for the ganache

- 250g (9oz) good-quality chocolate
- 125ml (4fl oz) fresh cream

what you'll need

- 2 x 20 cm (8in) sandwich tins
- baking parchment (optional)
- stand mixer (optional)
- heatproof bowl for bain marie or microwave
- spatula

1. Preheat oven to 170°C/325°F/Gas 3. Grease two sandwich tins or line with parchment.

2. Combine all the dry ingredients (the first five) in a large mixing bowl. In a smaller bowl, beat the eggs lightly, add the milk, oil and syrup and combine. Make a well in the centre of the flour mixture and add the wet ingredients. Mix well but do not over-beat: stick to about three minutes of beating by hand, or about a minute in a stand mixer. The resulting mixture should be quite runny.

3. Divide between the prepared sandwich tins and bake in the preheated oven for 20 minutes or until a skewer inserted into the centre comes out clean. Remove from the oven and leave the tins to cool on a wire rack.

4. Meanwhile, to make the filling, melt the chocolate, stirring periodically, either in a bowl in the microwave or in a bain marie (a heatproof bowl over a pot of simmering water). In another bowl, beat the icing sugar, cream cheese and softened butter together until creamy. Beat in the orange juice or Cointreau and add the melted chocolate.

5. Use a spatula to spread this mixture over the cake layers, reserving a little for the sides, and place one on top of the other to form a sandwich. Spread the reserved filling over the sides. Place in the fridge while you prepare the ganache.

6. Chop the chocolate into small pieces or melt it, as above. Bring the cream to the boil in a small saucepan, remove from the heat and stir in the chocolate. Allow to cool for 10 minutes before pouring over the cake to coat the top and sides. Return to the fridge for another 30 minutes to set.

7. Serve cold or reheated in the microwave for 20 seconds, with some ice-cream and some fresh fruit.

Great Aunt Ann's Chocolate Cake

ROSEMARY MCCONVILLE, CLONES GUILD, MONAGHAN

My mother used to bake this when I was a child. It's based on a recipe from her aunt Ann Simony. Ann went to work in Annamakerrig House as a young girl in the years between the two world wars and eventually became cook. A firm favourite with the Guthrie family, this cake was frequently served for afternoon tea. The beautiful old house is now the Tyrone Guthrie Centre where artists come to work in peace.

Serves 8

- 110g (4oz) soft margarine
- 110g (4oz) caster sugar
- 110g (4oz) self-raising flour
- 1 tablespoon cocoa powder
- ½ level teaspoon baking powder
- 25g (1oz) desiccated coconut
- 25g (1oz) ground almonds
- 2 large eggs
- 2 tablespoons milk, approx.

to finish

- melted chocolate or chocolate glacé icing (see below)
- walnuts or chocolate drops (buttons)

for chocolate glacé icing (optional)

- 225g (8oz) icing sugar
- 2 tablespoons cocoa
- 2 teaspoons softened butter
- 2 drops vanilla extract
- 2–3 tablespoons boiling water

what you'll need

- 18cm (7in) sandwich tin
- wire rack
- spatula

1. Preheat oven to 180°C/350°F/Gas 4. Grease and flour an 18cm (7in) sandwich tin.

2. Cream together the margarine and sugar in a large mixing bowl. Sieve the flour together with the cocoa and baking powder into a second mixing bowl. Mix the coconut and almonds into this flour mixture.

3. Beat the eggs well in a small basin. Add a little of this beaten egg to the creamed fat and sugar, then stir in some of the flour. Repeat until all the egg and dry ingredients are combined. The mixture should be a soft dropping consistency – you can add a little milk if needed to achieve this.

4. Transfer to the prepared tin and bake in the preheated oven for 20 minutes, which should give you a cake with a slightly moist centre. Remove from the oven and allow to cool in the tin before carefully turning out onto a wire rack to cool fully.

5. This can be decorated with melted chocolate or with chocolate glacé icing. If using the latter, sieve the icing sugar and cocoa into a mixing bowl. Add the softened butter, vanilla and boiling water and beat to incorporate fully*. Use a spatula to spread quickly over the top of the cake.

6. Once you have spread the cake with your chosen topping, you can add any decorations you fancy (such as nuts or chocolate buttons) and leave to set.

ICA Tip

*Alternatively, when making the icing, you could melt the butter before beating it into the sugar and cocoa mix, and add warm rather than boiling water.

Raspberry and White Chocolate Cake

MARY MANNERING, AGHABOG GUILD, MONAGHAN

White chocolate pairs beautifully with fresh raspberries, the tartness of the fruit cutting through the richness of the cocoa butter. Using good-quality ingredients really pays off in a simple recipe like this, as does having a bit of fun with the decoration.

Serves 8

- 225g (8oz) softened butter
- 225g (8oz) caster sugar
- a dash of vanilla extract
- 4 eggs
- 225g (8oz) self-raising flour
- 110g (4oz) fresh raspberries, halved
- 110g (4oz) white chocolate chips

for the butter icing

- 140g (5oz) softened butter
- 285g (10oz) icing sugar
- 1–2 tablespoons milk

to decorate

- whole fresh raspberries
- white chocolate chips

what you'll need

- 900g (2lb) loaf tin
- wire rack

1. Preheat oven to 180°C/350°F/Gas 4. Grease a 900g (2lb) loaf tin.

2. Beat the butter and sugar together in a large mixing bowl until light and creamy. Add the vanilla extract. Beat an egg in a small bowl and add this to the butter-sugar mixture, incorporating well before repeating with each of the remaining eggs one by one.

3. Sieve the flour into a separate bowl and then fold this into the wet mixture. Gently fold in the halved raspberries and white chocolate chips.

4. Transfer into the prepared loaf tin and bake in the preheated oven for about 45–50 minutes or until a skewer inserted into the centre comes out clean. Remove from the oven and leave on a wire rack to cool before removing from the tin.

5. Meanwhile, to make the butter icing, beat the butter in a large mixing bowl until soft. Add half of the icing sugar and beat until smooth. Add the remaining icing sugar and one tablespoon of milk and beat the mixture until creamy and smooth. If necessary, you can loosen the mixture further by beating in another tablespoon of milk.

6. Once the cake is fully cool, ice the top with butter icing and decorate with fresh whole raspberries and white chocolate chips.

Caraway Seed Cake

GERALDINE O'CONNOR, CLONES GUILD, MONAGHAN

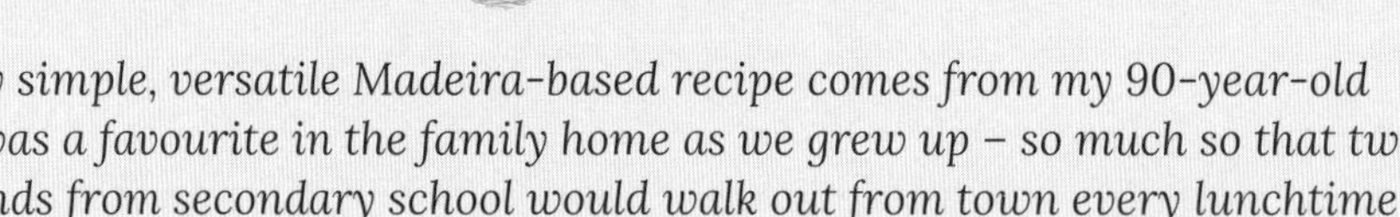

This very simple, versatile Madeira-based recipe comes from my 90-year-old mother. It was a favourite in the family home as we grew up – so much so that two of my friends from secondary school would walk out from town every lunchtime to meet me and get a slice of caraway, cherry or fruit cake from Mum. I like to think it was my company that they craved but I have a feeling it might just have been the promise of this delicious cake.

Makes one loaf or round cake

- 225g (8oz) softened margarine
- 175g (6oz) caster sugar
- 3 large eggs, beaten
- 100g (3½oz) self-raising flour
- 15g (½oz) caraway seeds

what you'll need

- deep 18cm (7in) round cake tin or 900g (1lb) loaf tin
- greaseproof paper or baking parchment
- stand mixer or electric whisk (both optional)
- palette knife
- greaseproof paper or baking parchment
- wire rack

ICA Tip

You can replace the caraway seeds with a handful of dried cherries or sultanas.

1. Preheat oven to 170°C/325°F/Gas 3. Grease an 18cm (7in) round cake tin or 900g (1lb) loaf tin and line the base and sides with a layer of greaseproof paper or baking parchment.

2. Cream together the margarine and sugar in a large mixing bowl until smooth.

3. Add a third of the beaten eggs to the creamed margarine, mixing to incorporate before sieving in a third of the flour and mixing again to incorporate. (This is best done in a stand mixer if you have one, or with a handheld electric whisk.) Repeat twice to gradually incorporate the rest of the eggs and flour, and then beat in the caraway seeds. Continue to beat for another couple of minutes to mix together well and make it light and fluffy.

4. Transfer the mixture into the prepared tin of choice. Smooth the top of the cake with a palette knife, leaving a slight well in the centre to allow the cake to rise evenly.

5. Bake on middle shelf of the preheated oven for 60–75 minutes or until a skewer inserted into the centre of the cake comes out clean.

6. Remove from the oven and allow to cool for 10 minutes in the tin. Turn the cake carefully onto a wire rack, remove the paper and allow to cool fully.

7. Store in an airtight container where it will keep for a few days. Enjoy a slice of this cake smothered in butter.

QUICK & EASY & QUICK & EASY

Simple Swiss Roll

JOSEPHINE HELLY, ICA NATIONAL PRESIDENT, GORT GUILD, GALWAY

This extremely straightforward Swiss roll recipe is a great one to have in your repertoire. It can be kept very simple with just a jam filling, or you can re-roll it with additional fillings such as fresh fruit and cream.

Serves 8–10

- 3 eggs
- 85g (3oz) caster sugar, plus extra to dust
- 85g (3oz) self-raising flour
- pinch of salt
- 3 tablespoons fruit jam

to finish

- extra caster sugar or icing sugar, to dust
- 125g (4½oz) fresh strawberries, sliced (optional)
- 200ml (7fl oz) fresh cream, whipped (optional)

what you'll need

- 33cm x 23cm (13in x 9in) Swiss roll tin
- baking parchment
- electric whisk (optional, but recommended)
- spatula
- clean, damp tea towel
- wire rack

ICA Tip

Fresh raspberries would also be lovely in this recipe in place of the strawberries, perhaps crushed gently and macerated in a little sugar with a little finely chopped fresh mint.

1. Preheat oven to 200°C/400°F/Gas 6. Line a Swiss roll tin with baking parchment. Use the tin to measure and cut out a second sheet, allowing at least an extra inch around the size of the tin.

2. Whisk the eggs and sugar in a large bowl until pale, fluffy and thickened. Sieve in the flour and salt little by little, carefully folding in each addition before you add the next. Use a spatula to spread the mixture evenly into the prepared tin and bake in the preheated oven for 10–12 minutes or until just firm.

3. Lay a damp tea towel on a work surface and place the second sheet of baking parchment on top. Dust with caster sugar.

4. Gently warm the jam in a microwave on a low setting for about 30 seconds, or in a saucepan with a tablespoon of water to loosen. Take care not to burn yourself with the hot jam.

5. When the Swiss roll is baked, remove from the oven and immediately turn out upside-down onto the sugared paper. Carefully remove the upper paper lining from the baked sponge.

6. Trim a strip of about ½cm (1¼in) from all four edges of the sponge – this provides a neat edge for your finished roll. Spread the loosened jam over the central area, leaving a border of about ½cm (¼in). Carefully lift about 1¼cm (½in) of the roll nearest to you and fold it over and away from you. Securing this folded end with one hand, use the other hand to bring the sugared paper over it. Now continue to roll the Swiss roll away from you, using the sugared paper as the guide.

7. When it is completely rolled up into a log, hold it in position for a few moments to help it set a little before carefully removing the paper. Gently lift the roll onto a wire rack, seam down. Dust with more caster sugar and allow it to cool fully and set.

8. If you want to add fresh fruit and cream, you can very carefully unroll the log once it is fully cool, and spread a layer of sliced strawberries and a little whipped cream over it, and then re-roll and dust with extra sugar. Serve cold, cut into slices.

Gluten-Free Sponge Cake

MARY O'HALLORAN, CLOONEY QUIN GUILD, CLARE

I am not coeliac but, like a lot of people today, I am gluten-intolerant. I love baking so I have adapted my recipes by swapping to gluten-free flours. I find that the resulting cakes are really light in texture.

Serves 8

- 3 eggs
- 110g (4oz) caster sugar
- 110g (4oz) gluten-free self-raising flour
- 1 teaspoon gluten-free baking powder

for the filling

- 300ml (10fl oz) double cream
- 4 tablespoons strawberry or raspberry jam

to finish

- icing sugar (see tip), for dusting

what you'll need

- 2 x 20cm (8in) round sandwich tins
- spatula
- palette knife
- wire rack
- electric whisk

1. Preheat oven to 180°C/350°F/Gas 4. Grease two 20cm (8in) round sandwich tins and line with parchment.

2. In a large mixing bowl, whisk the eggs and sugar for about five minutes until it is pale, light and fluffy and has tripled in volume.

3. Sieve in the flour a spoonful at a time, and gently fold in each batch with a spatula or wooden spoon before you add the next one, taking care not to knock air out of your whisked egg mix. It's important to take particular care with this step when working with gluten-free flour, which has an awkward consistency and more of a tendency to clump together than regular flour.

4. Divide the mixture between the prepared tins. Bake in the preheated oven for 20 minutes or until a skewer inserted into the centre comes out clean. Remove from the oven and allow to cool a little before loosening the edges with a palette knife and removing carefully from the tins. Allow to cool fully on a wire rack.

5. For the filling, whisk the cream until it forms soft peaks. Spread the base layer of cake with jam and top with whipped cream. Place the second layer of cake on top and dust with icing sugar.

ICA Tip

Note that not all icing sugar is coeliac-friendly, depending on the type of starch used to keep the sugar soft; so check the label if you want this recipe to be fully gluten-free (which cornstarch or tapioca starch are).

QUICK & EASY • & • QUICK & EASY •

Mystery Cake

ANNE HARRINGTON, BLACKROCK GUILD, DUBLIN

Shh ... don't tell anyone, but the mystery ingredient in this traditional American cake is the quite unlikely addition of a tin of tomato soup. The curious combination of ingredients makes a surprisingly good cake that happens to be vegan. This Depression-era recipe is proof that necessity is the mother of invention: the soup takes the place of milk or oil to bind the cake. Some versions would have used an egg or two, but this one doesn't. And the original would have used lard, replaced here by a choice of vegetable shortening or coconut oil, now widely available. Give it a go!

Serves 10–12

- 225g (8oz) self-raising flour
- 1 teaspoon bicarbonate of soda
- 1 teaspoon ground cinnamon
- ½ teaspoon ground cloves
- ½ teaspoon ground nutmeg
- ½ teaspoon salt
- 2 tablespoons (60g/2oz) vegetable shortening or coconut oil
- 225g (8oz) caster sugar
- 1 x 295g (10½oz) tin of tomato soup
- 125g (4½oz) chopped pecans or other nuts of choice, plus extra for decorating
- 140g (5oz) raisins

to finish (optional)

- lemon or lime icing (see page 104 or page 160)
- a handful of chopped nuts

what you'll need

- 23cm (9in) tube pan
- stand mixer (optional)
- wire rack
- spatula or palette knife

1. Preheat oven to 180°C/350°F/Gas 4. Grease a 23cm (9in) tube pan.

2. Sieve the flour into a bowl together with the soda, spices and salt. In a separate large mixing bowl or stand mixer, beat the shortening until soft. Sieve the sugar in gradually, mixing well before the next addition.

3. Mix about a third of the flour mixture into the sugar-shortening mixture, followed by about a third of the tinned tomato soup, beating until smooth. Repeat twice with the next two thirds until everything is incorporated.

4. Fold in the nuts and raisins. Pour the batter into the prepared tube pan and bake in the preheated oven for about 45–60 minutes, or until a skewer inserted in the centre comes out clean. Remove from the oven and allow to cool fully in the pan before removing carefully and transferring to a wire rack.

5. If topping with the optional icing, simply follow the instructions on page 104 or 160 to make the icing, and then spread it over the cooled cake with a spatula or palette knife, perhaps topped with a few extra chopped nuts. (For a non-vegan topping, you could also use the cream cheese frosting from page 184.)

ICA Tip

When an old recipe calls for 'shortening' it would have typically meant lard, but later recipes tended to replace this animal-based saturated fat with plant-based equivalents such as vegetable shortening or hard margarines. These can be high in trans-fatty acids or hydrogenated vegetable oil including palm oil, so some people prefer to opt for coconut oil as a natural alternative.

Scrumptious Carrot Cake

JOSEPHINE WHITMORE, CASTLEBRIDGE GUILD, WEXFORD

This three-tiered tower of a cake is a favourite of mine, which I first baked after recovering from an illness a number of years ago. My friend's mother had given me a magazine to keep me company while ill, and I found a version of this recipe in it. It is so easy to make, yet is guaranteed to impress family and friends.

Serves 12

- 225g (8oz) plain flour
- 225g (8oz) spelt flour
- 2 tablespoon ground cinnamon
- 1 tablespoon bicarbonate of soda
- 250g (9oz) unrefined caster sugar
- 300ml sunflower oil
- 4 large free-range eggs, beaten
- 1 tablespoon vanilla extract
- 425g (15oz) tinned pineapple, drained
- 300g (11oz) carrots, peeled and finely grated
- 100g (3½oz) walnuts, chopped
- 100g (3½oz) desiccated coconut
- 100g (3½oz) sultanas

for the frosting

- 285g (10oz) full-fat cream cheese
- 100g (3½ oz) butter, softened
- 100g (3½ oz) icing sugar, sieved
- 2 teaspoons lemon juice

to decorate

- 2 handfuls (25g/1oz) coconut flakes
- 1 handful 25g/1oz) walnuts, halved

what you'll need

- 3 x 20cm (8in) sandwich tins
- baking parchment
- wire rack
- spatula or palette knife

1. Preheat oven to 180°C/350°F/Gas 4. Grease three 20cm (8in) sandwich tins with oil and line the bases with baking parchment.

2. Sieve both flours, cinnamon and soda into a large mixing bowl, then mix in the sugar.

3. Add the oil, beaten eggs and vanilla and mix well.

4. Mash the pineapple with a fork or pulse in a blender to a rough purée (if using sliced pineapple, you'll want to finely chop it first). Add this to the bowl together with the remaining four ingredients, mixing well to fully incorporate.

5. Divide the mixture equally between the tins and bake in the preheated oven for about 30–40 minutes or until a skewer inserted into the centre comes out clean. Remove from the oven and leave in tins to cool for a few minutes before transferring to a wire rack to cool fully.

6. To make the frosting, whisk half the cream cheese together with the butter and icing sugar in a large mixing bowl before whisking in the remaining cheese and lemon juice.

7. To decorate, sandwich the three cakes together with a thin layer of frosting and stack them together. Spread the remaining frosting over the top and decorate with walnut halves and coconut flakes.

Whiskey and Salted Caramel Cake

EDWARD HAYDEN, ICA COOKERY TUTOR, GRAIGUENAMANAGH, KILKENNY

Edward Hayden is a chef and cookery tutor who has worked closely with the ICA for many years, presenting cookery classes and sharing his fantastic recipes. This rich cake is a little bit like Edward himself: generous, fun and a great addition to any social gathering!

Serves 8–10

- 175g (6oz) plain flour
- 1 heaped teaspoon baking powder
- 2 teaspoons ground ginger
- 1 teaspoon ground cinnamon
- ½ teaspoon ground cloves
- 175g (6oz) brown sugar
- 1 tablespoon Irish whiskey
- 2 large eggs
- 2 level tablespoons black treacle
- 200ml (7fl oz) milk
- 110g (4oz) butter, melted

for the salted caramel buttercream

- 110g (4oz) caster sugar
- 60ml (2floz) cream
- a pinch of sea salt, to taste
- 300g (10oz) icing sugar
- 110g (4oz) butter, softened

to decorate

- 50g (2oz) chopped hazelnuts

what you'll need

- 20cm (8in) cake tin
- baking parchment
- wire rack
- spatula or palette knife

1. Preheat oven to 180°C/350°F/Gas 4. Grease a 20cm (8in) cake tin and line with baking parchment.

2. Sieve the flour, baking powder and spices together into a large mixing bowl. Stir in the brown sugar and whiskey. In a separate bowl, beat the eggs together with the treacle and milk. Add the melted butter and mix well.

3. Make a well in the dry ingredients, pour in the egg and treacle mixture and mix until a smooth batter has been achieved. Pour into the prepared tin and bake in the preheated oven for 45–55 minutes or until a skewer inserted in the centre comes out clean. Remove from the oven and allow to cool slightly in the tin before turning out onto a wire rack and allowing to cool fully.

4. To make the salted caramel buttercream, heat the caster sugar and four tablespoons of water in a saucepan over a gentle heat, stirring until the sugar has dissolved. Increase the heat and cook the caramel, without stirring, for two or three minutes, or until golden and slightly thickened. Remove the pan from the heat and quickly whisk in the cream, taking great care as the caramel will be very hot and may splutter and boil up a little when you add the cream. Stir in the salt, pour into a clean bowl and set aside to cool.

5. Cream the icing sugar and butter together for at least four or five minutes, or until pale, light and fluffy, then beat in a tablespoon or two of the caramel for a smooth consistency.

6. Spread this icing over the cake with a spatula or palette knife, then drizzle with some additional salted caramel and some chopped hazelnuts.

ICA Tip

If you like, you could carefully slice the cake into two slimmer layers and sandwich these together with some of the icing.

Appendices

Glossary and Useful Equipment
Recipe Contributors
Acknowledgements

Glossary and Useful Equipment

A few words about temperatures and measurements

Please note that all temperatures given throughout this book are for conventional ovens. If you have a fan oven, reduce the suggested temperature by about 20°C (e.g. from 200°C to 180°C).

Note that all teaspoon measurements are for a level teaspoon, unless otherwise specified. All tablespoon measurements are for a level tablespoon, and not for a dessertspoon, unless otherwise specified.

Both metric and imperial measurements have been provided. It is best to follow one or the other, as in some cases they have been rounded up or down for practicality of use, e.g. 1oz = 28g, but the latter has been rounded down to 25g.

Glossary of baking terms

Activate: a term used in relation to a form of dried yeast called active dried yeast (see page 69) whereby the yeast must be rehydrated in lukewarm water and fed with sugar to activate it before use.

All-in-one: an extremely straightforward method of mixing a cake in which all the ingredients are quickly mixed together.

Bain marie: a system for cooking something in a container such as a bowl, where the container is set over boiling water to ensure a gentle cooking process involving indirect rather than direct heat; typically a heatproof bowl (Pyrex or stainless steel) is placed over a pot of simmering water.

Bake blind: to bake a pastry base prior to filling, in order to ensure a crisp rather than a soggy base. The base is lined with baking parchment and weighed down with dried baking beans so its shape is maintained.

Base-line: to line a cake tin with parchment to cover the base only.

Beat: the act of whipping or whisking a liquid ingredient such as cream or egg whites with a fork or whisk with the purpose of blending ingredients and/or introducing air.

Bicarbonate of soda: also known as sodium bicarbonate, bread soda or baking soda, this differs from baking powder and requires an acid such as buttermilk to activate its leavening properties (see page 69).

Bind: to moisten and bring together dry ingredients with a small amount of liquid in order to form into a paste or dough.

Blitz: to blend to a purée with a hand blender or in a blender.

Core: remove the centre of fruit such as apples, either with a sharp knife or melon baller.

Creaming: the method of mixing fat such as butter with sugar and beating them until they are pale and fluffy. The additional ingredient of beaten egg is then added incrementally and alternately to dry ingredients such as flour and any spices or flavourings.

Crimp: a term for impressing a patterned seal on a pastry rim; this can be done with fingers, fork or knife.

Crumb: a baking method for rubbing a fat such as butter into dry ingredients such as flour with your fingers until you have a crumb-like texture; also a bread term that refers to the structure of the dough once cooked.

Dropping consistency: a baking term for a consistency loose enough to drop from a spoon.

Fold: in baking, the gentle action of folding incorporates dry ingredients such as flour or sugar into whipped ingredients such as whipped egg white or cream while retaining as much air as possible in the whipped ingredients.

Knead: a method of stretching a dough in order to encourage elasticity and the formation of gluten; on a lightly floured surface, use the heel of your hand to stretch the dough away from you before folding it back over towards you, repeating for the specified duration.

Knock back: a step in bread-making that allows for the release of air trapped within a dough after the first proof or rise has taken place; this encourages the elasticity of the dough and can be as simple as folding the dough over several times or punching it gently with your fist.

Leavening: (or leavening agent) a substance used in baking to cause dough and cake batters to expand. Yeast and baking powder are leavening agents.

Proofing: to proof or prove a bread's dough is to allow it time to rise; during the first proof, the dough will typically double in size; the dough is then knocked back and allowed a second proof (often in the loaf tin) before baking.

Punch down: see knock back.

Quenelle: an oval shape made with dense semi-stable matter such as whipped double cream; created by moulding the matter between two spoons, or scooping with a single spoon preheated in hot water.

Sieve: (verb) the act of sieving (or sifting) dry ingredients such as flour or icing sugar removes any lumps that may have formed, ensures even mixing and distribution of dry ingredients and helps to introduce air into the batter.

Toast: nuts, seeds and spices can be toasted on a dry frying pan, under a hot grill or in a low oven in order to release aromas; watch closely to make sure they don't burn.

Whip/whisk: see beat.

Useful equipment

Baking beans: these dried, uncooked beans are used to weigh down pastry while baking blind (see glossary); the beans can be retained after baking for re-use.

Baking parchment: also known as silicone paper or baking paper, this is essential for many baking recipes in order to line baking tins; also useful for sealing jars of homemade preserves.

Baking sheet: a flat baking sheet (as opposed to shallow baking tray) is very useful for baking certain breads and cakes, and can be preheated for optimum results.

Baking tray: a shallow baking tray with a small lip that is typically used for roasting vegetables, fish or other protein but can also be used in place of a baking sheet, and can be preheated for optimum results.

Blender: a stand-alone electrical appliance used for chopping, mixing or liquidising foods.

Brown paper: useful for lining the outside of rich fruit cakes such as Christmas cakes in order to protect the edges from browning too fast. A double layer of parchment could be used in its place.

Bun tin: also known as a patty tin, this is a baking tray with six, nine or 12 cup depressions for making buns and mini pies.

Butter paddles: also known as Scotch hands, butter spades, butter pads, etc. These wooden spatulas were traditionally used to aid in the incorporation of salt into butter for the purposes of preserving the fresh butter and extending its shelf life.

Cake tins: Also known as cake pans, these baking tins come in various sizes and shapes. If using a square tin rather than a round one, reduce the dimensions by 2.5cm (1in). 'Cake tin' can also refer to the storage vessel that is useful for storing long-life fruit cakes, such as Christmas cake (see page 41).

Ceramic bowl: a traditional delph or ceramic mixing bowl can be useful for soaking ingredients overnight as it is less likely than plastic to absorb flavours and less likely than a metal bowl to react with the ingredients being soaked; also useful in pastry for its naturally cool properties.

Chef ring: a stainless steel mould used for various applications but useful in baking terms as a large cutter.

Chopping board: it is good practice to allocate one chopping board to dealing with raw meats and fish, another for vegetables including pungent onions and garlic, and another for fruits and bread. Always wash in hot, soapy water after dealing with raw meat and fish.

Cookie cutter: see scone cutter.

Cook's knife: a good, well-maintained knife will do much to improve your cooking; always store carefully to keep it as sharp as possible.

Electric whisk: a hand-held whisk useful for ingredients that need to be beaten for any duration; alternatively, see stand mixer or use a regular whisk and some old-fashioned elbow grease.

Flan tin: also known as a quiche tin or tart tin, it often has a removable base.

Food processor: a multi-functional appliance that has a container and a number of different removable revolving blades that allow food to be cut, sliced, shredded, blended, beaten or liquidised in the container.

Frying pan: whether you have a modern non-stick frying pan or an old-fashioned cast iron one, the weight of the pan is important; a heavy-based pan will distribute heat more evenly and be less likely to burn food.

Grater: a good grater is a real friend in the kitchen; look for one with several grades of fineness or invest in a selection of quality graters.

Greaseproof paper: a waxed version of baking parchment.

Hand blender: also known as a billy or stick blender, a hand-held electrical appliance is useful for liquidising, blending or puréeing foods, such as soups, without having to transfer them from the cooking vessel.

Heatproof bowl: when making a bain marie or double boiler, a Pyrex or stainless steel bowl will conduct heat better than a plastic or ceramic bowl.

Labels: essential for keeping track of frozen foods, which should always be dated and labelled clearly with details of contents; the same applies to homemade preserves.

Loaf tin: tins for bread-making (or loaf-style cakes) are usually defined by the volume they hold rather than their dimensions (e.g. 900g/2lb loaf tin).

Loose-bottomed tin: a baking tin with adjustable sides and a loose bottom that allow the cake to be easily removed once baked.

Measuring jug: a plastic, Pyrex or glass jug for measuring liquids; it is worth having both metric and imperial measurements on this, as well as American cups.

Measuring spoons: a stainless-steel collection of spoons, including teaspoons and tablespoons; useful to have for baking as many households no longer have a full-sized tablespoon in their cutlery set.

Melon baller: useful for coring fruit like apples and pears, though a sharp knife can do the job just as well.

Muffin tin: similar to a bun tin but deeper, this is a baking tray with six, nine or 12 cup depressions for making muffins.

Palette knife: useful for smoothing surfaces such as icing and for loosening and lifting cakes from baking tins.

Paper tin liners: made-to-measure liners for cake tins; useful to cut down on washing up and for the convenience of not cutting out baking parchment to fit your tin.

Pasta machine: comes in useful in baking when you need to roll a dough very thinly.

Pastry brush: useful for glazing cakes, breads and pastries; choose a silicone one, which is easy to wash.

Peeler: life is too short to use a bad peeler; there are various versions out there, so experiment; and when you find one that works for you, hold on to it.

Piping bag: handy for decorating cakes or cupcakes with precision.

Proving basket: specialist equipment for proving bread and worth investing in if you plan to bake yeast-based or sourdough breads on a regular basis, but not strictly necessary.

Ramekin: an individual round ceramic dish for making various pies and puddings.

Scone cutter: also known as a pastry cutter or cookie cutter. It is useful to have cutters in a variety of sizes for use in all sorts of baking. However, if stuck without one, a straight-rimmed glass can be used in its place.

Sieve: (noun) a wire or plastic mesh in a frame. It is worth having a general sieve for use with dry ingredients when baking, as well as a colander for draining wet ingredients, and perhaps a fine chinois for passing purées.

Skewer: to judge whether cakes and baked goods are fully cooked, a metal skewer can be inserted into the centre; if the skewer comes out clean, your cake is ready.

Spatula: a rubber 'spoon' spatula is useful in baking; it's handy for scraping down and incorporating ingredients that have stuck to the sides of a mixing bowl, as well as for smoothing a cake mixture into the baking tin. You may also need a separate flat frosting spatula or palette knife for icing cakes.

Springform tin: a baking tin with adjustable sides which allow the tin to be easily removed from a cake, once baked.

Stand mixer: a stand-alone electrical appliance with interchangeable blades and attachments; useful for everything from folding and whipping to mixing or even kneading.

Swiss roll tin: a flat tin with raised edges specially designed to bake a thin, rectangular sponge cake which then gets rolled up into a Swiss roll. It is also useful for making traybakes.

Tube pan: a specialist cake pan with high sides, a removable base and a central tube that encourages even baking and rapid rising thanks to the improved circulation of hot air through the central column; often used in airy cake batters that are at risk of collapsing, as the inner wall supports the cake's structure while it bakes.

Toothpick: can be used in place of a skewer for testing muffins and other small baked goods.

Twine: useful for securing a brown paper ring around a baking tin when slow-baking fruit cakes.

Rolling pin: a good rolling pin is essential for baking with pastry; some like to use a ceramic one to keep the pastry extra cool.

Weighing scales: if you like to bake, an electronic or digital scales is worth investing in, as it allows you to measure very refined and exact weights. These are reasonably priced and widely available.

Wire rack: this is essential for baking, generating the necessary circulation of air for forming a good crust on bread and for cooling cakes.

List of Contributors

The ICA would like to extend a sincere thanks to all the Guilds and individual members who shared their much-loved, tried and tested recipes with us all.

Ann Smith, Raphoe Guild, Donegal

Anne Harrington, Blackrock Guild, Dublin

Anne Gabbett, Mungret St Pauls Guild, Limerick

Anne McDonagh, Mullingar Guild, Westmeath

Annette Long, Castletroy Guild, Limerick

Anne Maria Dennison, Mainistir na Féile Guild, Limerick

Anne Rowlands, Fedamore Guild, Limerick

Astrid Moffett, Ballybay Guild, Monaghan

Ber Ennis, Horseleap Streamstown Guild, Westmeath

Betty Gorman, Castletown Guild, Laois

Breda McDonald, Mullinavat Guild, Kilkenny

Breege Lenihan, Ballinode Guild, Monaghan

Bridget O'Malley, Ardmore/Grange Guild, Waterford

Carmel Dawson, Ballyconnell Guild, Cavan

Carmel Garrett, Knocknacarra Guild, Galway

Caroline Power, Ratoath Guild, Meath

Catherine O'Dowd, Monaghan Town Guild, Monaghan

Claire Ann McDonnell, Moneystown Guild, Wicklow

Collette Dalton, Spa Fenit Guild, Kerry

Connie McEvoy, Termonfeckin Guild, Louth

Edward Hayden, ICA Cookery Tutor, Graiguenamanagh, Kilkenny

Eileen Bambrick, Drumboylan Guild, Roscommon

Eileen Redmond, Camross Guild, Wexford

Eilish McDonnell, Horseleap Streamstown Guild, Westmeath

Eleanor Calnan, Leap Guild, Cork

Elizabeth Murphy, Ballyroan Guild, Laois

Ethna Drudy, Frenchpark Guild, Roscommon

Eveline McCandless, Carndonagh Guild, Donegal

Frances Murray, Beltra Guild, Sligo

Geraldine O'Connor, Clones Guild, Monaghan

Helen Cronogue, Annaduff Guild, Leitrim

Helen Kavanagh, Borris-in-Ossory Guild, Laois

Hilda Roche, Ashford Guild, Wicklow

Janice Casey Bracken, ICA Cookery School, An Grianán

Janice McCandless, Carndonagh Guild, Donegal

Joan Dunne, Tradaree Guild, Clare

Joan Hayes, Crecora Guild, Limerick

Joan McLoughlin, Cappamore Guild, Limerick

Joan Noone, Blanchardstown Guild, Dublin

Josephine Helly, ICA National President, Gort Guild, Galway

Josephine Whitmore, Castlebridge Guild, Wexford

Kathleen Murray, Frenchpark Guild, Roscommon

Kay Devine, Bonniconlon Guild, Mayo

Kitty Harrington, Frenchpark Guild, Roscommon

Máire Uí Mhurchu, Cumann na Clochán Bréanain, Ciarraí

Margaret Ferguson, Horace Plunkett/ Dunsany Guild, Meath

Margaret O'Gorman, Camross Guild, Wexford

Margaret O'Hara, Bonniconlon Guild, Mayo

Margaret Redmond, Portlaoise Guild, Laois

Marie McCormack, Collinstown/Fore Guild, Westmeath

Marie O'Toole, Portmarnock Guild, Dublin

Marion Lawless, Portlaoise Guild, Laois

Marion Lyon, Maghera Guild, Cavan

Mary Fergus, Ballisodare Guild, Sligo

Mary J. Gallagher, Bonniconlon Guild, Mayo

Mary Mannering, Aghabog Guild, Monaghan

Mary O'Halloran, Clooney Quin Guild, Clare

Mary Timmins, Ballyconnell Guild, Carlow

Maura Walsh, Cappamore Guild, Limerick

Maureen Robinson, Horseleap Streamstown Guild, Westmeath

Michelle Early, Aughavas Guild, Leitrim

Miriam Murphy, Blanchardstown Guild, Dublin

Noeline Power, Tramore Guild, Waterford

Nora McKinney, Taughboyne Guild, Donegal

Patricia Cavanagh, Ballinode Guild, Monaghan

Patricia Gilligan, Sheelin Guild, Cavan

Patty O'Brien, Abbeyknockmoy Guild, Galway

Pauline McEnerney, Crosserlough Guild, Cavan

Rena McClean, Taughboyne Guild, Donegal

Rita Alves, Drogheda Guild, Louth

Rita Carolan, Clones Guild, Monaghan

Rosemary McConville, Clones Guild, Monaghan

Sarah McDermott, Ballinode Guild, Sligo

Sheila Baynes, Castlebar Guild, Mayo

Sue Wardell, Tinahely Guild, Wicklow

'Ballad of an Irish Wheat Field'

This traditional ballad was published in Maura Laverty's 1960's cookbook, Full and Plenty: The Complete Guide to Cooking. *I've always loved it and it seems a fitting ode to the natural ingredients at the heart of this book of bread and baking.*

Walk softly, O man, past an acre of wheat,
With awe in your heart and your face.
Walk humbly, O man, and with reverent feet,
For strength slumbers here – Can't you feel its heart beat?
And beauty's own couch is an acre of wheat,
And holiness dwells in this place.

Breathe gently, O breeze, on the grain-heavy ears,
That drank long and deep of spring rain.
O breeze, ripple gently the yellow-tipped spears.
Our little ones, caught in the rush of the years,
Need growth that is stored in the wheat's golden ears
All mother-ripe now with smooth grain.

Sing sweetly, O birds, as you skim the rich field,
And sprinkle your hyssop of song,
For here in each silken-caped kernel is sealed
The secret of living. The liberal yield
Will strengthen and quicken, O birds of the field,
And comfort the earth's hungry throng.

Shine kindly, O sun, keep it warmly alive.
On this field lay a tender caress,
For here is the reason men struggle and strive
And strain, sweat and anguish and battle and drive.
And life's spent for wheat just to keep men alive.
O sun, let your rays kindly bless.

Walk softly, O man, past an acre of wheat,
O birds, mute your silver-splashed mirth!
O breeze, hold your breathing! O sun, shed your heat!
For here is the food that God gave us to eat ...
The Body of Christ comes from sanctified wheat,
Twice-blessed be this fruit of the earth!

ANNETTE LONG,
CASTLETROY GUILD, LIMERICK

Acknowledgements

There are always many people to thank when a collaborative work of this type is produced and as with our previous books, I would like to say a big thank you to all the brilliant members of the ICA who contributed to this collection of delicious recipes and tips. The members have excellent skills and without their input we would not have a book of this calibre.

I would also like to thank the staff of the ICA Central Office – Rebecca Ryan, Anna Sinnott and Nora Naszalyi – for their administrative work and the collation of the submissions.

And finally, to our editor, Aoife Carrigy, to all at Gill Books and to the team who worked so effectively in creating another beautiful book of which the ICA and the members can be very proud: photographer Leo Byrne, food stylist Charlotte O'Connell and designer Tanya Ross.

Thank you all,

Josephine Helly

National President of the Irish Countrywomen's Association

Index

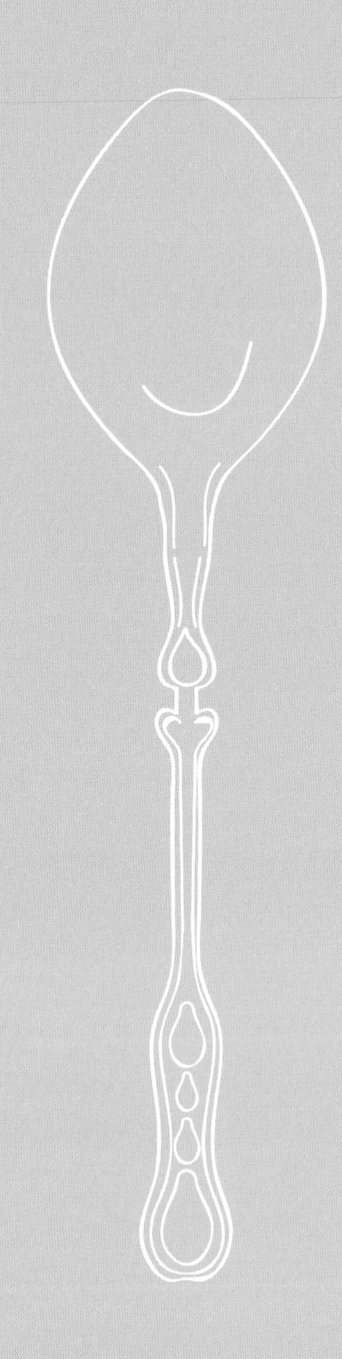